REFLECTIONS

Lessons for Life from the Man You Are Becoming

AUTHORED BY **SPENCER GESWEIN**
EDITED AND IMPROVED BY **MANY**

FOREWORD BY **ANDREA BRACKETT**
ILLUSTRATIONS BY **TEKOA**

WESTBOW
PRESS®
A DIVISION OF THOMAS NELSON
& ZONDERVAN

WestBow Press books may be ordered through booksellers or by contacting:

WestBow Press
A Division of Thomas Nelson & Zondervan
1663 Liberty Drive
Bloomington, IN 47403
www.westbowpress.com
844-714-3454

ISBN: 978-1-6642-3101-6 (sc)
ISBN: 978-1-6642-3102-3 (hc)
ISBN: 978-1-6642-3100-9 (e)

Library of Congress Control Number: 2021907571

Print information available on the last page.

WestBow Press rev. date: 05/20/2021

This book is dedicated to my father, Paul Geswein, and others like him. Our problems would be fewer and our days richer should more of us embrace their teaching and lessons for life.

Thank you, Dad.

CONTENTS

FOREWORD

MY ASSOCIATION WITH THE MAN WHO INSPIRED THIS BOOK GOES BACK twenty-seven years, when a small motorcycle pulled into the driveway of our just-bought hobby farm in central Indiana. After introducing himself and exchanging pleasantries, Paul Geswein said, "Let me know if there is anything we can do to help." His son Spencer quotes this line in his book. Anyone who has ever met Paul probably has heard him say this, but, unlike some who might offer help, not ever thinking they'd actually be called upon, Paul really hoped to be enlisted—and in my family's case, that help was needed right away, and plenty of times since.

We needed a pond, we needed a concrete floor in our toolshed, we needed raccoons removed from the walls of our ancient farmhouse, we needed a corncrib to be "shoved in" and hauled away, and we needed basic overseeing as we stumbled through the early days of managing our little farm. It turned out that Paul was one-stop shopping when it came to all of these projects, and he did them all with the trademark Geswein commitment to excellence you will read about in this book. His face was often inscrutable, the mark of a great poker player and salesman, both of which he is. When I ran over a pile of barbed wire I had just collected, or when he was called upon to rescue some piece of machinery I had dumped into the pond, he didn't double over with laughter until the crisis had passed and the situation was mended.

Paul and his wife, Pam, and my husband, Boone, and I became close friends, sharing family gatherings and outings to local eateries such as the Tastee Treet and The Farmers Table and working on farm projects. Our backgrounds seemed different, but our life lessons and experiences seemed all too familiar, and we could laugh at ourselves and have the kind of no-holds-barred conversations that refresh the soul. I already knew Spencer was a chip off the old block, but when we had to sell the farm after twenty wonderful years, and Spencer and his wife, Tekoa, became the buyers, my confidence in his integrity and sensitivity reached a new level. He helped me sell off vehicles, tools, and furniture, refusing to take any commission, and also gave us a generous offer for the farm that was easy to accept. He made the transfer a pleasure rather than a sorrow.

This book is a great read—often funny, sometimes tragic, always earnest, always honest. It demonstrates that idealism is not dead. Follow on Spencer's ride from boyhood to midlife, and you will encounter characters you wish you would have met in your own life, people who either challenged or mentored Spencer, or both, and who helped mold him into the man he is today.

An important subplot of the book is to thank each and every one of these sterling examples of humanity. In addition, Spencer invokes words of wisdom from the Bible and from thought leaders who have inspired him, including some famous names and some not-so-famous others we might all like to get to know: Zig Ziglar, Dave Ramsey, Admiral Wm. H. McRaven, and Orrin C. Hudson, among others.

Spencer's gift for storytelling lends this memoir the air of an adventure. Whether applying for top positions in college and in work or racing across America "Cannonball-style," Spencer gives it his all and doesn't waste a minute. You won't be surprised when you learn that, two hours before his wedding, he was prepping and polishing a Mustang Cobra R for a burnout following the ceremony. You'll laugh—and shake your head—at his car-buying exploits, and you'll delight in his telling of finding his true love and raising a family.

This book is more than a memoir, though. It is a clarion call to become a better person and to build a better life for yourself and your family in our confusing times. As you read, you will want to stop frittering away time and money, and, critically, you will want to support your family better and treat everyone around you with greater empathy and gratitude. You will want to walk more closely to God, or at least start hoeing in that direction, beginning with the Golden Rule, which, in his youth, Spencer heard his father repeat almost daily.

Spencer doesn't believe in coincidences, and neither do I. Though time and distance could have been an easy excuse to let our friendship lapse, something sustained our connection and led to my involvement in this book. I'm honored and humbled to have been a small part of this project. Particularly, I'm in awe that Spencer was able to write a book with three children still at home. It makes me question my excuses and makes me want to answer his call to "do my best." Sign me up, Spence.

Andrea Brackett
Dunnington Road, fall 2020

ANDREA BRACKETT AND I, 2017

REMINDERS AND GUIDEPOSTS FOR THE JOURNEY

Character (noun): the mental and moral qualities distinctive to an individual
Constitution (noun): composition with respect to morals, health, and strength
Courage (noun): resolve in the face of fear, pain, or grief
Grit (noun): courage and resolve; strength of character
Manliness (noun): the traditional male quality of being brave, strong, and vital
Mettle (noun): vigor and strength of spirit or temperament
Moxie (noun): force of character, determination, or nerve
Patriarch (noun): a male leader, often sought, respected, and held in high esteem
Swagger (noun): a distinctly confident, often arrogant, walk or manner
Virility (noun): the quality of having strength, energy, and a strong sex drive

"If a man writes a book, let him set down only what
he knows. I have guesses enough of my own."
—Johann Wolfgang von Goethe

"I'm not telling you what to do; I'm just telling you what I know."
—Wise Old Farmer

"If you don't have anything nice to say,
don't say anything at all."
—Dad

DAD AND MY CREW—
THANK YOU

I AM A MAN OF RICH BLESSINGS AND GOOD FORTUNE. THIS MUCH I know. I have had many good people willing to pour their lives into mine, to support and enrich me in many ways. They have helped forge the man I am today, and they continue to refine and improve the man I strive to become. Topping that list is my father, Paul Geswein, "Dad" to me, "Papaw" to his grandkids, and "Wally" to his brothers and many friends.

Through stories and reflections of life, I would like to share a bit about my dad, about his spirit and character, and about his love and leadership, which established my trajectory and continue to illuminate my steps. A strong, supportive crew moves in and out of these reflections as well, each teaching, helping, and caring enough to shepherd me along life's journey. I am grateful to each and every one.

Though these lessons are introduced and described mostly through my own life experiences, I've made no attempt at an autobiography. Please continue reading in that spirit. My reflections pull together a collection of lessons for life—timeless wisdom delivered by Dad and other teachers as their student became ready. They are intended to remind and challenge readers to imbibe the lessons and live life in a full, impactful, positive way. This book is an inadequate but well-intentioned way for me to say thank you and publicly commit anew to life's higher standards, their standards.

PAUL GESWEIN, CIRCA 1950

If you know my father personally, or any of the characters who have earned a place in this book, you are fortunate indeed and will likely nod and smile with familiar appreciation as you read. These are salt-of-the-earth people. We need more like them. If these folks are new to you, through my reflections, I hope to introduce you to them and bring you closer to both them and their enduring lessons for life. I hope you enjoy coming to know Dad and my crew. Odds are, you know people like them. Like me, perhaps you will be inspired and encouraged by their examples and lessons. Perhaps you will find new hope and new opportunities to serve and perform at your own highest level.

My mother was a wonderful woman, not to be overlooked. She sacrificed for, and contributed to, my first thirty-nine years in many ways. Without Mom, I would not have life, might not have adequate empathy and balance, and likely would not strive toward excellence in some of the areas I do today, most notably in reading and writing. In April 2010, barely sixty-seven years young, Mom killed the cancer ravaging her body as she drew her last breath. I trust my phraseology is not lost on the careful reader, particularly those who have been touched in some way by cancer. My words represent a sanitized gesture bidding angry farewell to this evil disease. One way or another, we win. Cancer is ultimately defeated.

Mom is home now with the Lord and other loved ones who proceeded and followed her in death. I appreciate my mother. I miss her. I wish she were here to help complete and share this book with me. She would have proofed my work and corrected many things. She would have recognized and supported its thankful intent, but she would not have wanted me to share it beyond those directly involved. She would not have been comfortable with publication.

My mother avoided controversy like the plague, you see. By Mom's thinking, bold statements of conviction, conservative activism, conspicuous disruption of cultural currents, prayer before meals in public places, and anything unlisted that might draw unwanted attention was to be minimized, avoided altogether if possible. She was a great mom and a strong, intelligent woman but not one to engage in a battle that didn't directly affect her children.

Mom was not a stirrer of the proverbial pot. In the right circumstances, for the right reasons, I, however, can be. Some readers may find elements of this book controversial or offensive in content but never in language. That's okay. I believe good-willed people can be bold without being belligerent and can disagree without being disagreeable. Thank you to each and every reader, regardless of persuasion, for your time and consideration.

There are other women in my life who are also beloved, strong, contributory, and irreplaceable. Elevated among them are my wife, Tekoa; our daughter, Sterling; my sister, Sherry; my cousin, Cindy; and my late grandmothers, Helen and Gladys. I thank each of them here and now. Possibly another book, more feminine perhaps, should follow this one to reflect on their many kindnesses, strengths, and positive influences and to extend more thorough thanks to them and others I have missed. For now, though, I must focus and get *this* book to the finish line.

My book has indeed reached the finish line and is before you due in no small part to the patience and support of my family. It is before you in a form that is logical, readable, and grammatically correct due largely to my editors Andrea Brackett and Scott Kays.

As you will soon read, Andrea has been a treasured friend and supporter of my family and me for many years. The contribution and improvements she brought to this book are considerable, and I am deeply grateful. In Scott Kays, I am delighted to have found a new friend and future editor. Our work together on this book almost didn't happen. That would have been a small tragedy. I can't speak highly enough of how thorough and professional his editing services have been. I thought I was detail oriented! Scott is a consummate professional at the highest level and a stellar guy with many interesting tales of his own. His editing services through Azami Press have made this book far better, period. I can say with confidence that any errors remaining are mine, not theirs. Thank you.

We press on. This book, this time, these reflections are directed toward Dad and other strong characters, mostly men, whose power of word and example have been immensely helpful to me. Now is the time to reflect and double down on their teachings. Now is the time to acknowledge and thank them, to glean from them ever more. Now, not tomorrow. Tomorrow may never come; today is all we have.

MY STRUCTURE, *OUR* COLLECTIVE CONTRIBUTION

REFLECTIONS, MOSTLY CHRONOLOGICAL, EBB AND FLOW AS LIFE FOLLOWS its course. As need arises, brief sidebars are included to expand upon important lessons, to share some humor perhaps, or maybe to vent frustration in the direction of a sympathetic ear on matters dear to me and pertinent to the topic at hand. As reflections become current, we are left with some poignant reminders that life on earth is neither fair nor forever.

Coming into the book's final chapter, the reflective, appreciative message is stirred about and fanned into a rallying cry to those concerned with the sorry state of our nation. With each passing day, there is mounting disdain for God and the Judeo-Christian, character-based values upon which this country was founded, values upon which Dad and my crew built their lives, careers, and families.

From bases such as these, I extend a call to timely, positive action that drives change. We must each get about our business with a bit more focus, a bit more bravery and moxie, perhaps. We must do our part right now to love, to live, and to leave our legacies of eternal value. Your work and positive contribution are desperately needed.

You are needed now!

Within and around our families, our nations, and our world, too often can be found expanding decadence, an abundance of needless suffering, a shortage of hope, and a hunger for quality leadership. To be sure, solid leadership and lives of high standard are still on display daily, even among our youth; however, I feel they are becoming more the exception than the rule. Perhaps I am not alone with this foreboding feeling. Perhaps more than a few readers agree with me that, in spite of valiant efforts and shining lights in some areas, our trajectory is perilous and our steps on the way of excellence are burdened by the sheer numbers of people who see or accept things differently. I appreciate the hopeful guidance for life offered to young folks by author, speaker, and chess champion Orrin C. Hudson: "Heads up, pants up, grades up, and never give up." There is something in Mr. Hudson's words for all of us.

God's plan for restoration includes both you and me. It starts with each of us individually. Our own houses must be in order. From within, restoration must find traction and build momentum. It must expand into our circles of influence and snowball. You and I must positively affect our families, friends, loved ones, and those in our communities as my dad and this crew have done for me. No one else can do our proverbial push-ups. No one else can be expected to apply and to teach the lessons that have been delivered to us. They are ours to manage, ours to build upon and convey.

"Much will be required of the person entrusted with much, and still more will be demanded of the person entrusted with more."
(Luke 12:48)

We have been entrusted with much. We owe it to ourselves, to our children, and to our grandchildren to deliver our very best. A renewed focus on, and commitment to, biblical wisdom and character-based action is needed, a focus and commitment as found in the stories you will soon read. It is a focus and commitment that loves and considers neighbor just as much as self. Dad's translation of the Golden Rule from the seventh chapter of Matthew's Gospel is the cornerstone. This guidance I've heard thousands of times in my youth. "Do unto others as you would have them do unto you." —Dad

Thank you for reading my simple book, for reflecting on the blessings and the blessed in your own life, and for doing your part to influence and serve those around you with grit, mettle, and excellence. As I embark, I am reminded of two thoughts that might prove helpful.

First, in his thick Austrian accent while delivering one of his numerous speeches on success, Arnold Schwarzenegger once challenged his listeners to think deeply about their lives and trajectories: "*Who* do you want to be?

Not *what*, but *who*?" Mr. Schwarzenegger was not asking his listeners what career they wanted to pursue or whom they idolized. Rather, he was inviting them to search the recesses of their souls, to decide what type of person they longed to be. He was asking what their actions and their lives should stand for, what legacy they wished to leave behind. Mr. Schwarzenegger's question bears repeating and thoughtful consideration as we are needled to attention by these reflections and lessons. *Who* do you want to be?

Finally, this oft repeated guidance from Dad casts me off: "Son, if it is worth doing, it is worth doing right. Do your best."

Whom Do I Reflect?

In my physical reflection, I don't see my dad clearly except for a few features here or there. I'm taller and leaner than he is. His structure is heavier and more compact. His hands and bones are bigger. His legs are much shorter and his nose broader. Dad is not a hairy man. The hair he does have is collected on his head, much as it has always been, with a nice, distinct flow and a stable line. Even in his mideighties, Dad's hair remains somewhat dark. He passed this hair stuff on to me. While I am thankful, I suppose, to have Dad's hair, skin tone, and a few other observable features, I am more appreciative of other attributes, which are of higher value, both physical and nonphysical. There is something in the eyes, something in the jawline, something in the set of his shoulders and mine. There is something in how I walk and talk the way he did in earlier days. There is something of confidence and constitution that we share. Pride and protection of name and family, a desire to stand firm for something, a resolve to do good and right by others and by God—toward such things we have no choice but to strive, even if we fall pitifully short at times.

As I reflect more mentally now than physically on my life and Dad's, and on the lives of those cherished members of my crew, distinct elements of shared character come into focus. Dad, and each of these others, is unmistakably present in soulful ways, allowing this physical man to stand erect and move forward boldly in spite of my many shortcomings, weaknesses, and vices. Dad's legacy, and the legacies of these other mentors, continues to take shape in me and in many others they have influenced. Their legacies will endure long after they have left us for their eternal homes.

PAUL GESWEIN, CIRCA 1955

Dad is a patriarch, a rock for me and many more. He has always been a strong man's man, a definitive alpha male. I make this statement without reservation or apology. There is nothing wrong with being an alpha male despite what popular culture suggests. Being an alpha male can be admirable, something of which to be proud, not ashamed. Dad is, and will always be, an alpha male, no matter what drain, pain, illness, or unkind challenge comes with advancing years or disease. Steadfast strength and resolve, without fear or complaint, is what is expected from an alpha. Dad delivers.

Zig Ziglar correctly recognized that a strong father is often the first god a child knows. Such was certainly true in my case. Dad was something of a god. As an adult, I know clearly that Dad is not a god, nor would he want to be thought of in that way. There is only one God, not my dad, and certainly not I. Dad is a treasured father, a rock-steady example of thoughtful, strong, faithful male leadership, regardless of advancing years and Parkinson's disease. I want Dad to hear, and to know, that whatever positive traits I possess are largely because of him and the path he began crafting for me more than a half century ago. Whatever negative traits I possess are because of me and the vices in my life over which I have not yet triumphed.

"Train a boy in the way he should go; even when
he is old, he will not swerve from it."
(Proverbs 22:6)

On many occasions in my youth, often cast toward my older brother, who was in the midst of something ornery, Dad would say, "Son, you sleep in the bed you make for yourself." While so true and applicable, equally true and thoroughly understood by Dad is the fact that we are all imperfect, sinful humans. Despite good intentions, we fail more often than we like to admit—Dad, too. The apostle Paul struggled similarly: "For I do not do the good I want, but I do the evil I do not want" (Romans 7:19). Recognizing frailty, but coaching toward virtue, Dad also reminded and encouraged me, "God doesn't expect perfection. He looks for faith, and He expects persistence. He expects you to fight the good fight and never give up." Deflating as it may seem, we may carry some of our earthly struggles to the grave. In our final hours, we may still be battling. As long as we struggle constantly forward, never embracing whatever our vices might be, we will have fought the good fight and finished well. Such is the persistence God expects.

I am a work in progress, and I will not give up. There is much for me to improve.

Thankfully, Dad and most of the characters in these reflections are still here and available, poised to encourage, guide, and serve as they always have. Please do not misunderstand, however. They will not always be. As you read and reflect in your own way about loved ones and mentors in your life, I encourage you to develop a sense of urgency as I have.

If there is something you need to say, someone you need to love or forgive, something you need to learn, someone you need to teach and encourage, or some wrong you need to correct, do these things now! All we have with certainty are the moments immediately before us. These should be wasted neither on lamentations of the past nor on aspirations for a future we are unwilling to construct by our actions. The number of our tomorrows is finite. Get busy and don't waste time in transit.

CHAPTER 1

THE EARLY YEARS

Lessons on Practical Skills, Personal Durability, Safety, and Parenting

I WAS BARELY FIVE YEARS OLD, AND DAD WAS PREPARING TO DROP A LARGE, dead hickory tree at the edge of our yard. I sought shelter and Dad's approval within the walls of a doghouse not far away, a doghouse that Dad had built years before. No ordinary doghouse, this was instead a scale model of the house our family lived in. Dad and his brothers built our family home with their own hands—many hands. That's what men did in his day. They did whatever job needed doing, and they did it well. Dad was the fourth of seven boys in his family. Together with my grandpa, over the course of about ten years, four of his seven "boys" built houses for five of their families and one home for a friend of the family.

Each of these houses stands firm and is in good repair at the time of my writing. Construction took place in the gaps. Each of these men had other functions, including farming, school, or other employment. Dad was transitioning from high school into early adulthood at this time. Each man knew a fair amount about every trade, and each had particular skill in at least one area. Together, Grandpa and these four sons covered all the trades. They constituted a full crew. Dad did much of the masonry and concrete work. My uncle Bob, the kingpin and Dad's oldest brother on the crew, was a multitalented, natural leader. He was a stoic, deadpan craftsman with plenty of ingenuity. Bob didn't have an engineering degree, and he didn't need one.

Back in the confines of my well-built doghouse, peering out at the condemned tree and the unfolding events, I was as carefree as a child could be. I neither recognized potential danger nor appreciated my father's skill with a chainsaw. I didn't comprehend that the activity even required skill. I simply recall the satisfaction I had in knowing that Dad approved of my shelter and its placement relative to the massive tree. I was enthralled by the sound and the effectivity of the machine and the man who wielded it. With amazed eyes and eager anticipation as wood chips flew and the tree began to lean, I could barely wait to yell, "Timber!" at the moment of truth. I was a happy boy in good hands.

My siblings and I, loaded for a "horsey ride" on Dad, circa 1971

Dad played with me and my siblings in our youth, seldom missing an opportunity to teach. He was an engaged father and an active participant, the kind who was more likely in the midst of a game, on the floor, or in the sandbox rather than in his recliner in front of the TV. He could hit a baseball higher, sling a Frisbee longer and flatter, and chuck each of us along grander flight paths in a swimming pool than any human I ever saw.

Physical strength, bravery, and courage Dad possessed aplenty. He faced opposition one way: head-on. It didn't matter if the opposition was inanimate or human, warm blooded or cold. Never did he encounter a jar lid he couldn't open, a lug nut he couldn't break loose, or a log he couldn't split. We appreciated the fact that Dad was intolerant of foul behavior and profanity in the presence of his wife and children and that he was not opposed to confronting offenders. On one particular family vacation, when I was perhaps eight or nine years old, I remember standing in line for some ride or attraction when it became impossible to ignore the foul mouths of a group of early high school boys next to us in line. Dad drew the attention of the group and asked that they clean up their mouths so that others didn't have to hear that sort of talk.

Amid their smirks, annoyed looks, and muffled comments, one of them decided it would be a good idea to rub his nose conspicuously with his middle finger. Dad came close to the edgy youngster's face, looked him right in the eye, and engaged, "You think I don't notice your foolish gesture there, tough guy? You and your little friends need to…" I lost what remained of the conversation as Mom pulled my siblings and me her direction, away from the excitement. Nothing developed. The teens decided it might be better to watch their tongues, terminate their games, and stand down.

I also remember riding with Dad on several occasions, pulling into the driveway of a friend or potential customer, and being "greeted" by an unknown, overly protective farm dog. Dad would continue undeterred, paying little attention to the dog. He would get out and direct me soundly, "Stay in the car," as the door shut. He would not hesitate. Rather, he always walked directly to his destination, letting the dog worry for itself. He was wise enough not to look the dog in the eye but courageous enough to proceed as planned, prepared to fight if needed. He never needed to fight. No dog ever messed with him. There was little fear for the dog to smell but its own.

Courage is not the absence of fear but resolute motion toward an objective in spite of fear. Dad faced things head-on. In the "my dad is stronger than your dad" spars of boyhood, I was quite confident. Dad was invincible. He was a man among men.

In his own youth, Dad was an excellent baseball player. A stocky, pain-tolerant, work-hardened farm kid, Dad was pulled forward as a freshman to catch on the varsity team. As a junior in high school, he once swung at a pitch with such intensity that when he missed, his feet tangled as he attempted to collect himself. He fell awkwardly, still grasping the bat. The fall dislocated his thumb. Once back to his feet, Dad was met between the batter's box and the dugout by a coach who assessed the injury. His coach decided to relocate the wayward thumb right then and there. Dad proudly recalls stepping back to the plate, hitting a double on the very next pitch. Dad coached several seasons of Little League as my brother and I moved through. He was delighted with my interest in—and aptitude for—catching. I knew that the tenacity and the scrap I brought to my game made him proud. Baseball and work connected us.

In my earliest, fondest memories outside of baseball, I was outside, in Dad's shop, in the woods, around our pond, in the yard, simply in Dad's presence, learning, doing, cleaning, building, and repairing. Just *being* with Dad, spending time with him, busy and active on anything, contributed to a wonderful, memorable childhood for me. Strange as it may seem, I even enjoyed pulling gunk out of the pond. For the uninitiated, pond gunk is an odiferous, gelatinous, sometimes sharp combination of moss, large branches, small twigs, pond slime, and excrement from fish, frogs, turtles, and the like. Occasionally, one might also find fishing lines, lures, bobbers, chip bags, and cigarette butts from inconsiderate fishermen. We regularly extracted this tasty stuff, laid it on the bank for a few days to dry, then gathered it into a pile to burn later. We would use a sturdy steel rake to reach out into the water to pull or float a collection of gunk to a point of leverage where we could lift it out completely with the rake or reach our hand into the slippery mess for a better pull.

Extracting pond gunk was not for the faint of heart, the sensitive, or the sanitized. Snowflakes need not apply. If you thought your world would end if a willow branch flicked wet, fermenting goo across your face, you had no business extracting pond gunk. Pond gunk helped put some of life's unpleasantries into proper perspective. It helped purge fragility and replace this unproductive trait with the more desirable quality of personal durability. Somebody has to do it. You aren't going to break or die. You don't need gloves and a hazmat suit. Get over it. Dig in there and get the job done. Such was Dad's lesson, and those were the days. I wouldn't trade them.

Toasters, mowers, flat tires, shed roofs, leaking faucets, plugged drains, or cantankerous go-karts—it mattered not what; Dad fixed what needed fixing. It seemed Dad was able to fix almost anything with the most basic of resources. He owned only a spattering of poorly matched tools, saws, and drills. His work benches and cabinets were recovered from various renovation projects or were purchased for cheap as scratch-and-dents from the hardware store. He managed to make it all work reasonably well. He made do. A fully stocked rolling Snap-on tool cart Dad did *not* have.

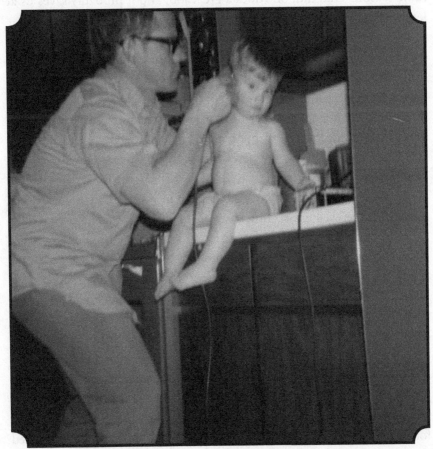

DAD CUTTING MY HAIR, 1972

Dad was even a skilled barber because hair needed cutting on a regular basis, just like the grass. I recall sitting on the kitchen counter as Dad cut my hair every few weeks. There was no need to pay a barber; that would be foolish and wasteful. Dad was good. Our cuts were timely, tidy, and precise. Dad cut our hair for years. I have no memory of anyone else cutting my hair until I was at least ten or eleven. The girls started paying more attention to me and my hair, so I did, too. I'm sure Dad shook his head and laughed a bit in those preteen and adolescent years, confident that the years of vanity would pass. They did. Today, though it matters little to me in the grand scheme of things, I guess I am thankful that I have hair. I am also more than happy that my wife cuts my hair and the hair of our two sons for the same reasons Dad did. She does a great job, and it probably saves us at least $60 per month.

Dad let us do our own stuff, too. He encouraged it. He knew that we learned by doing, even when we made mistakes, *especially* when we made mistakes. The first construction project of my own that I can remember involved disassembling a wooden fence from the backyard and reusing the materials to construct a shelter for our recently acquired 4-H hogs. Dad looked ahead approvingly at my plan: "There is the saw. Here are some additional nails. You already have your source of wood. Good luck. Let me know if you need anything."

At that time, kids weren't protected from every sharp edge and hot surface. We mowed grass, climbed trees, split wood, ran chainsaws, built fires, and shot BB guns and small rifles. Goodness, we climbed trees *with* chainsaws if that's what was needed. It often was. We didn't own a polesaw. For all I knew, they didn't even exist then. I was the family monkey with a saw in those days. I still climb trees carefully with a chainsaw today when my polesaw is not available. Harnesses or climbing gear? No, we didn't have that stuff. Your safety gear was between your ears. Most of my generation is still here today, none the worse for wear, perhaps as much a testimony to sound judgment as to good luck. Dad knew each of us kids was clever and had a keen sense of self-preservation. He knew we would learn to think things through, take precautions where needed, and ask for help if something felt too risky. The fact that Mom usually preferred staying inside was also a great enabler.

SIDEBAR 1:
SAFETY

Please don't take the wrong message away. I am a firm believer in operating in a safe manner with the right equipment whenever possible. Proper safety precautions and safety gear are very important. However, without first having a well-developed sense of self-preservation and good judgment, all the safety gear in the world is unlikely to prevent you from hurting yourself or others. I work in many environments with equipment of all sorts that can cause injury if not handled and deployed properly. Tree care using chainsaws is, and has always been, one of my favorite environments. Eye and ear protection are musts, and quality chaps are a good call in many cases. Vision and hearing cannot be replaced, and chainsaws can inflict mortal wounds in fractions of a second if one is not careful. Never skimp on safety in these areas.

Literally just a few short months ago, I was provided with an excellent example worthy of elaboration and sharing. For the first time in my life, no exaggeration, the first time ever, I called a tree service for help. I needed to remove three large branches way up the side of a mighty oak. These three branches were staggered up the tree's trunk from thirty to fifty feet high and were each at least a foot in diameter at their bases. The branches would have impeded the clean fall of a nuisance tree nearby that needed to come down. This nuisance tree was hanging precariously over my house, and its roots were beginning to cause problems for the sidewalk and basement walls. It needed to come down safely without falling on any part of the house or perimeter fencing.

My older son and I studied the situation and considered options and alternatives thoroughly. It seemed like forever, probably over an hour, that we pondered and pondered uncharacteristically. We studied the lengths of our straps and polesaws. We changed our ladder positions numerous times. We considered and reconsidered our climbing gear. We even considered dropping the oak altogether so that its branches were no longer in the way. We certainly did *not* want to give up and spend the money for a bucket truck. But, I decided that none of our options, creative and plausible though each might be, was safe enough. Our ladders weren't tall enough. Our climbing gear was not adequate, and we knew better than to think the nuisance tree would miss the house if we just left the oak alone and gambled. None of this was worth the risk. Our safety was more important, and we weren't going to sacrifice the entirety of this beautiful old oak tree just because the nuisance tree had to come down.

I called the folks with the right equipment, and we shuffled the activities of our day to perform other work while we waited on the professionals to arrive with their bucket truck. Thirty minutes after they arrived and $200 later, the oak branches were safely on the ground, and my son and I were able to proceed with dropping the nuisance tree without risk of damage or injury. It was the right call, and it was the right bit of instruction by example for our adolescent son when he needed to see it. Do what you have to do using the right equipment, the right protective gear, and plenty of good judgment.

> Be neither sidelined by fear nor crippled, literally,
> by foolishness. Safety is important.

SIBLINGS, BIKES, AND BB GUNS, 1978

Before stepping away from the topic of safety, I should acknowledge the fact that parents can only do so much. They can't be everywhere with their kids 100% of the time. Our life experiences draw from many sources, including family, friends, teammates, etc.

If you are fortunate enough to have siblings, you know that they provide a wide array of valuable fodder for life and opportunities for learning. I love my older brother, Shawn, and my sister, Sherry, very much and am blessed to have them. Shawn and I, as brothers often do, shared many experiences and survived many things that should have caused us more harm. Older brothers are highly effective teachers, for better or worse. Here are just the first few of many reflections I could draw from this cavernous well.

Shawn and I used to set up ramps to jump our bicycles, sketchy ramps at best of concrete blocks and scrap lumber. For bragging rights, we would build maximum speed and see who could fly the highest, the farthest, or both. Eventually, when regular flight lost its luster, one brother would lie down physically under the flight path while the other brother sailed over top with nary a concern. Plans like these were fun and exciting until they weren't anymore, such as when the jumping brother missed the ramp entirely and crashed into the unsuspecting brother lying prostrate, causing anguish for both.

When two-wheeled antics got boring, we sometimes agreed to shoot stuff. Out came the BB guns and more grand ideas. I am pretty sure Shawn had a BB lodged in the palm of his hand for years that ricocheted off a glass mirror in the trash that we attempted to shatter by shooting repeatedly. No safety gear or glasses, just two young boys having fun, indirectly learning about life and its dangers.

In reflecting on such experiences, I can't help but shake my head, recalling the old adage "It's all fun and games until someone loses an eye." Thankfully, we didn't. I allow a grateful smile to trim my shaking head, quite aware and appreciative of the fact that we did indeed emerge largely unscathed.

Some of life's most effective lessons, however, are indeed cast with pain as the main ingredient. I vividly recall the first time we sampled chewing tobacco, Beech-Nut, I believe, the full-leaf, in-your-cheek sort. It was beneath a tree in the front yard of our neighbor's farm. This man was a chewer, a younger man, but a man nonetheless by our standards of the day. He was short and stocky and had a Tom Selleck swagger and mustache. He drove not a Ferrari but a Jeep, and he seemed cool with his cheek full of tobacco, projecting black spit whenever, wherever, he wanted. Ironically enough, I believe his name actually was Tom.

Unopposed to introducing two youngsters to his nasty habit, Tom poked the aromatic open pouch silently in our direction with a nod of his head and an inviting lift. I think I hurled within two minutes. Shawn turned several shades of green but lasted a bit longer. There is a great scene in the movie *Secondhand Lions* where Walter is first given the opportunity to chew. This scene reflects our shared experience surprisingly well.

Our chewing experience must not have been enough to learn all we needed to know about tobacco. We had more to learn. In our youth, Dad smoked. We wanted to give smoking a try, but we weren't about to ask Dad if we could try one of his cigarettes. We were pretty sure he would say no. We heard somewhere that corn silks could be dried and smoked just like tobacco. Being country kids in Indiana, we had plenty of silks available. Foolish as we were, we smoked these dried silks in homemade "cigarettes" constructed of lined notebook paper held closed by clear tape. Mom and Dad might have known. I'm not sure. If they knew, they allowed our foolishness to build to a crescendo where a valuable lesson could be administered to maximum effect.

On one occasion, Shawn decided to fill a pipe he found with dried silks, or whatever other dried vegetation we could gather together from the woods, fields, or roadsides. He began to smoke it secretly near an open window in our basement. Mom's keen nose quickly sniffed him out, literally. Mom didn't bark or lecture incessantly. Rather, she led him straight up to the back patio and directed him to sit on the seat of the lawn mower. There on the mower, she made him continue smoking the rest of that pipe *and* all the other dried stuff he had collected until he was good and sick. I looked on, not needing to endure the pain of that lesson personally. It was enough for me to watch his anguish. I never had another thing to do with smoking or tobacco in any form. Thank you, Mom, and thank you, Shawn. Sorry about your luck, Bro. Dad also kicked his smoking habit around that time, never to return. Perhaps Dad learned a lesson that day, as well.

I include these reflections with considerable caution, to teach and to keep things real in this sidebar on safety. My choices of experiences to share are not made out of pride or for any sort of honor. On the contrary, if there are any children reading or being read to, please understand and don't duplicate our mistakes. We benefited from our mistakes not because they were cool or glamorous but because many of them hurt, sometimes badly, and we resolved never to repeat them. Please learn these lessons through our experience and your careful attention, then move along. There are enough mistakes out there that each of us will make in the natural courses of our lives that we don't need to knowingly replicate those we've heard or read about. Please listen and steer clear.

With great sincerity and contemplative spirit, I remind myself, and urge each reader, to carefully consider these words from one of my favorite poems, which is often credited to Rev. Claude Wisdom White, Sr.:

A Little Fellow Follows Me

A careful man I want to be,
A little fellow follows me;
I do not dare to go astray,
For fear he'll go the self-same way.

I cannot once escape his eyes,
Whate'er he sees me do, he tries;
Like me he says he's going to be,
The little chap who follows me.

He thinks that I am good and fine,
Believes in every word of mine;
The base in me he must not see,
The little chap who follows me.

I must remember as I go,
Through summer's sun and winter's snow;
I'm building for the years to be
That little chap who follows me.

In light of the poem, does this photo need
description? My young nephew Aaron and I, 1993

Back safely and happily to other lessons and loves of youth, I fondly
recall lawn mowers, go-karts, dirt bikes, three-wheelers, utility tractors,
snowmobiles, heavy equipment, and automobiles. We were always operating

something. I loved it all. I was often in the catbird seat, i.e., Dad's lap. I was given limited control of the sticks and steering wheels of bulldozers, backhoes, motor homes, go-karts, and the like from this position when I was very young. Dad was calculated and empowering. He taught us respect and responsibility by example and by giving us the reins. We learned under his watchful eye by doing, by feeling responsible, by considering the pitfalls and the risks, and by feeling our way forward through the fear.

On one particular occasion, I remember steering the motor home in traffic from Dad's lap in the mountains of North Carolina. There were orange construction barriers on one side and tractor trailers on the other. I remember thinking this felt a little risky, a little scary, but also "a lot" exhilarating. "Just focus and relax; you are doing fine." Dad's quick hands were hovering, ready to correct any deficiency in wisdom or steering that he saw brewing. He was shaping my skills, building my confidence, indirectly developing my worldview.

Dad's philosophy is more challenging to apply in today's culture, but certainly not impossible. These days, a worrisome neighbor and a simple phone call might spawn a lawsuit or bring police and child protective services to your door. My wife and I have some experience in this area. Stay tuned.

I'll conclude with one face-contorting recollection from early childhood that has to do with my occasional reluctance to eat all the food Mom made. We didn't waste much in our family, certainly not food. Mom was an excellent cook, but that doesn't mean I always liked everything she prepared. Dad's position was simple: eat everything on your plate. He worked hard to provide it; Mom worked hard to prepare and serve it. He reminded us that others would be grateful to eat the food we wanted to throw out. Mom often interceded quietly after Dad finished his meal and left the table to tend to dishes. That was Dad's practice and his contribution. Doing dishes helped Mom with dinner cleanup, and it helped get rid of grime under Dad's fingernails from the day's work—win-win.

Back at the table, Mom would make little deals with us, drawing a dividing line with our fork through a dollop of cottage cheese or a spoonful of green beans. She would quietly say that we had to finish the right half or the left half or whatever. Perhaps we might have to eat at least three pieces of those horrific purple beets. Mom loved beets. For me, they elicited a similar reaction as did that awful chewing tobacco. Why would anyone who wasn't starving eat beets? Dad was the straightforward disciplinarian. Not always, but more often than not, Mom was the softy.

SIDEBAR 2:

PARENTING

Parenting is difficult, and every child is different. These are true statements. Equally true is the fact that, no matter the child, no matter the situation, no matter the approach, in the final analysis, *every* child needs discipline. As his parent or guardian, as long as he is under your care, *you* must always be the boss—always. Solomon's wisdom from the proverbs has much to offer in this area. In my opinion, some of the most fitting guidance comes from the thirteenth chapter and twenty-fourth verse of the book of Proverbs: "He who spares his rod hates his son, but he who loves him takes care to chastise him."

Notice the words *hate*, *love*, and *care*. Solomon's choice of words is very important. Some readers may recoil at the usage of the word *hate* in this translation. Please understand, however, that, in this usage and context, Solomon is referring to hate not as something evil or malicious but rather as the opposite of love. To hate is perhaps to willfully withhold love or to fail to provide love when and where love is needed most. Solomon does not encourage parents to beat or brutalize their children. Rather, out of immense love, the caring parent is to apply chastisement and correction at the right time and in the right situations, using considerable care, because he loves that child enough to do what is best for him, regardless of comfort or convenience.

A few other translations attempt to be kinder, gentler, clearer perhaps, such as the Contemporary English Version, which states, "If you love your children, you will correct them; if you don't love them, you won't correct them." The God's Word Translation actually uses the word *spank*. Yes, *spank*. Using clear language and telling the truth today, calling a spade a spade—amen to that!

Rarely, but occasionally, a timely, stern spanking will do wonders for a wayward child. In most cases, it will stop the problematic behavior in its tracks and will not be needed again. More subtle forms of correction will likely be adequate in the future. Again, in this proverb, Solomon is not suggesting regular verbal or physical abuse, not even close. Rather, he is reminding parents of the often-difficult responsibility they have to love and care enough for a child to reprimand and provide suitable course corrections when needed. Unwillingness to provide stern, loving correction amounts to abandonment of that child in his time of need.

Our society is laden with spoiled phone-wielding kids, violent video games, overpriced fashions, foul mouths, and entitled attitudes because somewhere along the line, most likely early in the process, there was a parenting breakdown, and the child became the boss. Don't let that happen in your family, and don't be deceived into believing that your children want you to be a pushover. Parents, fathers especially, please listen carefully. Your kids don't want you to be weak. Children will test you, but they don't want you to fail the test, even though their actions suggest otherwise. Deep down, what kids really want and need is your resolve, your strength, and your protection. They want to feel completely protected and secure. That's what their little tests are really digging at. When you fail their tests, when you cower or cave and deny them the discipline they need, they lose faith and confidence in you as their provider and protector. They know instinctively that if you won't stand firm against their simple little tests, then later, when the stakes are higher, and the proverbial wolf is at the door, you won't stand before that test, either. You won't provide the protection and security they need.

You don't have to be male. You don't have to be physically strong. You don't have to have powerful hands or a deep voice. You must, however, have fortitude and resolve. Even though Mom was softer than Dad, Mom had plenty of resolve of her own, and she knew when to bring her teammate into the picture if she ever needed his help. She seldom did. Together they were an effective discipline duo. They never beat, abused, or verbally reduced any of us. We just knew our limits. If it ever got to the point where Dad grabbed hold of your upper arms, clamped you motionless following an impactful, attention-getting jolt, and spoke some correction directly into your eyes through a nearly locked jaw, you knew you had run afoul in some significant way. You needed to alter your way, never to return, and you needed to make the change immediately. We never had any doubt but that our parents were in charge of our household. I received a spanking only once in my life, and I've only delivered a few to our children, who are now grown past that point. Stern, loving discipline works. Provide it.

You are the boss. Be the strong, loving, caring, discipline-providing parents your children need when they need you.

Before leaving this sidebar, I would like to offer a few thoughts and share a related story pertaining to the role of grandparents on the landscape of a child's discipline. While it is important that grandparents concede the lead role to parents in providing discipline, there should be no mistake that grandparents still have an important role to play and that they should strive to play it well. Grandparents need to let the parents be the parents and should do their best to be supportive of the disciplinary approach taken by the parents in most cases. Yes, it is certainly fine and natural for grandparents to be a little easier, a little less restrictive perhaps in this area of the child's life. They should not, however, back away completely and become pushovers, providers of excess, or enablers of poor behavior.

With those statements, I let this topic rest since I am not yet a grandparent. I don't want to overstep my bounds or my experience. I can confidently say, though, that Dad is, and Mom was, welcome support in ensuring adequate discipline for our children. Dad clearly defaults to my wife and me, but he is neither a pushover nor an enabler. His grandchildren know and respect this.

It was the late 1990s or early 2000s, and I was at my sister's house helping Dad on some building project. It was a nice day. We were outside at work on whatever the project might have been when my mom emerged with grandson Colton. At the time, Colton was perhaps three or four years old. A very bright child, Colton was not easy to raise in those years. He could be as sweet as pie, or he could be a pistol. He also gravitated distinctly toward Grandma. Grandma was very loving and fairly easy on him.

On this particular day, Grandma must have needed to tend to something else, so she brought Colton out to be with "the boys" as we worked. She sent Colton out into the garage with clear instructions to be careful and to be "a good boy." "Well, hello, Colton! Good to have you join us," Dad said as he continued working. More for Colton's hearing than for Grandma's, Dad went on to say more softly, "Oh, don't worry, he'll be a good boy. He knows that if he isn't a good boy, Papaw will swat his little bottom and set him straight."

Colton slowed down, studied the scene intently, and considered his options carefully with a pensive look. He was calculating probability and risk. Contemplation didn't take long. His countenance relaxed as he reached a conclusion. He did an about-face back into the house. He knew that Papaw was kind and welcoming but that Papaw was true to his word. To be clear, Colton's return to the house wasn't one of sadness over lost opportunity or another in a long string of rejections by beloved Papaw. No, young Colton was bright enough to know that he had no intention of behaving adequately to avoid discipline, and he willingly chose a less confining environment. More than twenty years later, with much love and many course corrections, Colton has emerged as a solid young man and Christian leader.

CHAPTER 2

GROWING TOWARD MANHOOD

Lessons on Work, Workmanship, Materialism,
Enjoying Life, and Moving with Purpose

DAD SURVEYING, CIRCA 1960

MEN HAVE BEEN DESIGNED AND BUILT FOR WORK AND CONQUEST FROM
Adam's earliest days in the garden. Author and psychologist Dr. Emerson

Eggerichs refers to this nature as the "instrumentality of the male." According to Dr. Eggerichs, "It is part of the very warp and woof of his being." For as long as I've been alive—and since his own youth, I'm sure—Dad has been filled to the brim with a drive to work both physically and financially. As long as work doesn't interfere with faith or family obligations, if there is work to be done, that's where you'll find Dad, even today. Throughout his prime earning years, Dad made and saved money at rates, and in quantities, that those outside the family never knew. He taught us to work hard, to make plenty of money, and to invest and spend money wisely. For Dad, work wasn't primarily about the financial gain. It had more to do with applying an honest effort, doing your best at whatever your task might be, and completing work of value. Work was about taking pride in accomplishment, reaching objectives, and reflecting happily on the other side. When it came to possessions and provisions, our family had enough. We didn't need anything fancy. We weren't trying to impress anyone. We just needed "functional". Sometimes the word functional was interpreted broadly.

We did not have air conditioning growing up. We didn't have it at home or at church, and it was seldom used in our cars if they had the feature at all—often they didn't. Windows and fans ruled our days. You positioned your bed under a window with the door open so that cool evening air provided natural comfort for sleeping. Our home had a large fan in the ceiling of the hallway between our bedrooms. The sounds of the louvers moving, the drone of the big electric motor, and the welcome draw of cool summer air are refreshingly vivid yet today.

We only had two cars: Mom's bigger, nicer car and Dad's smaller, simpler one. We used them both plenty, but unless there was good reason for using Mom's bigger car, like going to church or to some other more formal function, our family often squeezed into Dad's smaller car to save fuel. We didn't die from insufficient elbow room or tarnished images. We didn't need the biggest or the best. Whenever our family enjoyed nicer things, which we certainly did from time to time, it was always clear that these were wants and desires, little splurges. It was fine to enjoy the nicer things on occasion, but they were not to be mistaken for needs. They were paid for, in their entirety, with disposable cash. Besides the homestead, nothing was ever purchased in small bites or with credit. I really never even heard of consumer credit until I went to college, but I do remember seeing the final mortgage check Mom wrote for our homestead. We lived on sixteen beautiful acres with a three-acre pond in a comfortable, well-built, handcrafted home. I was nine. Dad was only forty-three.

What I did hear often was "Work first; play later," which applied equally to physical *and* financial disciplines. If your work wasn't done, you wouldn't waste your breath asking to play. If you didn't have the money, you didn't buy it. That seemed simple enough. Dad's clear but seldom-verbalized lessons about money included these: work hard, save, invest, make do, and spend smart. Impress others with your work, not with your stuff.

Over the years, Dad grew and transitioned his primary career from heavy-equipment operator, to land surveyor, to real-estate broker, and finally to crop-insurance agent. He was always looking for opportunities to provide more for our family. In the extra moments, Dad trimmed shrubs, mowed grass, split and delivered firewood, surveyed farms, and sealed driveways to fill any financial gaps or save for those little splurges.

Work hard and manage money wisely.

Some of my fondest memories from early adolescence are those working with Dad. It was mostly quiet companionship, learning by watching and imitating, participating in many of Dad's gap-filling ventures. Sparse words of teaching and course correction came along the way. The work was always directed toward accomplishing something worthwhile to which we could turn and gaze with pride once completed. Dad shared with me the pride he always felt looking back at a cord of wood split and neatly stacked, a driveway beautifully sealed, a shrub carefully crafted, or a waterway graded to perfection. He took pride in telling his waterway customer that he could drive his truck down that waterway just as fast as he wished. Dad had attended to every detail of the job. He had applied passion to his craft, and his product was as flawless as humanly possible. Not only would that waterway flow water smoothly down its center, but its edges were works of graded art, as well, without a rock or a ripple. Dad understood and carefully guarded the fact that his name, and the name of his family, stood on the quality of his work. He did his very best to present both his name and his work unblemished. Dad is a man of simple excellence and honor.

DAD'S GRADED PERFECTION, CIRCA 1959

SIDEBAR 3:

QUALITY AND WORKMANSHIP

Dad's example inspired my own work. Our working relationship grew stronger with the accumulating years. Later in life, his example prompted me to coin my own quality-accountability reminder: "Passion is in the details." There can be a considerable difference between getting something done by meeting the minimum requirements and getting that same job done correctly, completely, and with a passion for excellence that proclaims, "That's mine!" This passion for quality, for excellence and attention to every detail, applies to all areas of life, not just to our work lives. It applies to finances, to relationships, to faith, to recreation—you name it. Passion matters.

It is akin to a positive mental attitude, perhaps. I like what Zig Ziglar had to say in this regard: "Positive thinking won't let you do anything, but it will let you do everything better than negative thinking will." Can't the same be said for a passionate commitment to quality, workmanship, and personal excellence? For example, piles of wood and stacks of wood are quite different from each other. The same can be said about a pile of money differing from a stack of money. The quantities of wood and currency in each collection may be the same, regardless of form, but their handling and arrangement suggests much more.

Piles suggest carelessness, lack of order, and likely waste or loss. A careless woodsman who fails to elevate, stack, or at least cover his firewood is likely to find it damp, degraded, and unable to provide life-giving heat in his time of need. In a similar way, perhaps more clearly, modern or urban readers can envision the inflated then deflated lottery winner whose pile of empowering cash, at first joyously abundant, dwindles to mere coinage by frivolous behavior and ride-along "friends."

PILE   STACK

Stacks, on the other hand, suggest order, care, attention to detail, stewardship, and preservation. Passion can be found in the details of everything we do if we take care to infuse it. "If a job is worth doing, it is worth doing right," Dad would often say. While the casual observer may never attend to your products or services closely enough to notice the passion you've built in, you'll have the satisfaction of knowing it's there and that you did your best. The careful observer, however, along with our ultimate Judge, will notice and appreciate your extra effort and the investment of your talents in both the modern and the biblical sense.

Advancing dutifully each day with our best efforts and with our best investments of self is worth it. While we are here, we will enjoy the respect and admiration of friends, colleagues, and customers. More importantly, when our day comes, we will hear the coveted welcoming words of heavenly reward and celebration from Jesus's parable of the talents in the twenty-fifth chapter of Matthew's Gospel: "Well done, my good and faithful servant."

Dad performed most of his work with a passion for quality long before I ever adopted the phrase "Passion is in the details." Notice I said, "Most." There were times, and there were projects, where Dad would say, "That's good enough." It was Dad's way of shutting down operations that didn't justify additional investment of time or resources. Understandably, truncation of this sort was more common when there was more work to be done than could be accomplished in the time available. Dad had no problem moving on and directing effort to things with greater priority or greater importance.

One example might be washing a larger or older vehicle such as a farm truck. For Dad, if time was limited, you might just skip the roof, or you might get it mostly dry and then move on. By his way of thinking, you don't see the roof, and it won't be long before the old truck is dirty again anyway, so why waste the time if time is short? Another example might be selectively mowing a yard with areas of grass that grow fast and other areas that grow slowly. Dad might "peak-shave," or just mow the tall spots for the time being and then leave the rest for next week to save a few minutes and some mower fuel. The grass would need mowing again soon, so just hit the high spots for now and move on. The whole yard could be mowed next week once it was all tall. Worded differently, the same philosophy was imparted to my fellow engineering classmates and me many years later as we approached graduation as seniors: "Gentlemen, you need always to remember whether you are engineering a grand piano or a park bench." —Dr. Owens

These days, Dad's "good enough" approach is often applied when folks are doing something for him and he wants to be respectful of their time. He wants to avoid putting them out in some way. He doesn't want to be a burden on their time, which he respects as limited and valuable. While I understand and appreciate the logic and sentiment behind the "good enough" and "park bench" philosophies, this is one life path that I have chosen not to travel as regularly as the others.

For me, it is very difficult to leave a job without each practical detail being completed to my satisfaction, even if time and resources are limited. I believe every element of the job reflects my values and my commitment. They are elements of my signature. It is one of the reasons it took me more than five years to finish this book. I find it difficult to move on, to "stick a fork in it." I am content going overboard in pursuit of perfection, even though I know I'll never actually achieve perfection. If I'm going to be accused of something, I can think of many things worse than being accused of being a perfectionist—at least as it relates to work. Perfection will never be achieved, but we are likely to get much closer to excellence if perfection is our target.

I recently was confronted with this question: "If you could do better, should you?" It is a great question that plays perfectly to this topic. There are times and seasons when we must stop. What we have done will have to be good enough. Perhaps we may, in fact, be out of time or resources. The final bell chimes, and the test must be turned in. Winter winds blow, and harvest must stop. Our physical strengths and aptitudes wane, and we must accept our limitations. I had to finish this book. In another five years, this group may be smaller, and I may have missed my chance to say thank you. Regret may displace opportunity. There are many other times and seasons, however, when we can do better. We may not be unduly limited by time or resources. I contend that, when circumstances are flexible, our answer to this question should always be "Yes, we should do better." If we opt to watch TV, just loaf around, or perhaps move on to the next project that we only intend to approach with a portion of our best selves, we are doing an injustice to ourselves and everyone else invested in us, including God. If you could do better, should you? Yes, you should whenever you are able.

How you do anything is likely how you do everything.

1. Your work quality speaks volumes about you. Do your best.
2. If time is limited, and it usually is, use time wisely on things that matter most.
3. Work quality, like quality of character, is a result of choices you make constantly. Make good choices. Neither your character nor your work will ever be perfect, but the tireless pursuit of perfection brings you closer to excellence.
4. On occasion, it is okay if you do not follow in the exact footsteps of treasured leaders. Make sure the path of your departure is moral, ethical, and well calculated. You may end up being wrong, or you may set a new high bar that inspires others. Keep moving forward.

Dad gave me great examples and taught me to stand on my own two feet, making my own decisions, even if those decisions differed from his on occasion. Good parents don't seek to raise clones. They seek to develop the best fully functional adults they can. They are always educating, inspiring, and attempting to steer their children and others toward success and away from the challenges and pitfalls they wish they could have avoided.

Moving purposefully to the next topic, I'll say that Dad was never slow or slack about anything. He walked fast and did not restrict his pace on my account. I was to keep up, even if I had to jog. He wasn't being inconsiderate, irresponsible, or abusive. On the contrary, he was teaching and challenging me by way of speedy, silent example. Occasionally, Dad would pull me out of elementary school to help him on survey jobs that required lots of walking, placing and pulling metal survey pins, steadying survey rods to plumb, winding metal tapes, and moving trucks and equipment. Dad walked so fast. I mostly jogged. He never spoke about his walking pace, but his example turned me into a fast walker. In college, with friends trying to keep up, I would justify my pace: "Life is short; don't waste time in transit." The enduring words of the great Coach Wooden, "Be quick, but don't hurry," would have found a receptive ear with my dad.

The concepts of quality and prompt action bring me to another frequent Dad phrase from my youth. This was a phrase you never wanted to hear: "Here, let me do that for you." It meant that you had failed, not because you were unskilled or unable but because you *decided* to fail. You chose sloth and/or mediocrity over excellence and honor. If you had a job to do, you were expected to get it done correctly and promptly. If you failed to perform in either of these areas, you didn't fear physical reprimand; you feared being on the receiving end of this phrase. Without another word, Dad would provide the example and the discipline you needed, along with a healthy dose of embarrassment, by grabbing the rake—or jumping on the mower or snatching the trash bag or whatever else had been your task—and taking *his* time to complete *your* task. He required merely a fraction of the time it would have taken you. He completed the task properly while you hung your head with embarrassment and ever-observant eyes.

Thankfully, I didn't hear that phrase often, but when I did, I recall that I might have opted for a spanking instead. "Here, let me do that for you" made you feel guilty beyond measure for your laziness, your shoddy work, or both. The modern articulation of authors and speakers Orrin Woodward and Chris Brady, "Do it. Do it right. Do it right now," is rooted in the same soil as Dad's lesson of getting after our business at hand with purpose.

I opened my first savings account when I was no more than seven years old. Kids could do that in the 1970s, and I was aggressive just like Dad. Saving was an indirect and moving target for me. I loved to accumulate money, not for the love of money or for the sake of its material equivalents but for the love of the accomplishment that produced the money. Money is a lousy measure of success in some areas of life, but in other areas, it can serve as a reasonable indicator of progress.

By age ten, I led a small crew of my buddies in picking up rocks from the fields of a local farmer. Dad dropped me off in the farmer's barnyard on his way to work. I arrived clean, dry, and fresh at 7:00 AM with my snack box. He picked me up again dirty, wet, and tired at noon. With a John Deere 4020, my buddies and I spent these early days of the summer scouring the fields for rocks and debris, depositing each load in piles beyond the end rows of the field. We would stop briefly around 9:30 to dip into our boxes for a drink and a snack to keep us energized. We would often take our break eight or ten feet in the air, perched in the bucket of the tractor among the branches of a mulberry tree to add some fruit (and protein-filled microscopic insects) to our diets. Dad was proud. I was proud. The work was honest, and, at $25 per day in 1981, my savings account was growing nicely.

Though Dad earned good money and saved and invested wisely, he was not opposed to spending some measure of disposable income to enjoy life in the moment. In early adulthood, Dad owned two Corvettes. The first was a red 1963 convertible, which Mom spun out on a slick winter road and crashed into a road sign. The second was a white 1965 coupe. He bought both of these beautiful cars brand new with cash. To this day, Dad proudly recalls that he paid $5001 for the '65, the highest-priced car that had ever come through our small-town dealership up to that time. These beautiful Vettes lasted just a few years each until family and business took center stage. Dad is not one to preserve and protect his personal pleasures to the detriment of his family. He sold the '63 within twelve months of being repaired from Mom's crash, and he sold the '65 when my brother and sister (twins) arrived in 1967. I don't know what became of the '63, but after being sold, the '65 died a grizzly death, along with its new owner, who lost control on a high-speed corner and launched both of them into a tree.

29

DAD GOLFING, CIRCA 1980

Not to be without some personal pleasures, Dad also loved golf. Thankfully, this hobby actually contributed to his business. He was a scratch golfer in his prime and conducted much business on the course. Naturally, a country-club membership became one of his profitable, indulgent pleasures. Dad was hopeful that I would develop a love for the game of golf as he had, but it was not to be. I played well in a couple of youth tournaments but never did so with passion. The game is too relaxed and leisurely for me. I always enjoyed the time with Dad and the challenge of seeing how hard I could hit the ball, but that's where it stopped.

Our family enjoyed camping and travel, as well. Mom and Dad were wise enough to invest in these experiences when the time was right. My siblings and I fondly recall many local camping trips and one multiweek summer adventure out West, where we took in the Cheyenne rodeo, the Badlands, Mount Rushmore, and the beauty of Yellowstone. There were four families on this particular trip. We hauled a trailer full of bikes, another trailer full of rafts and river equipment, and motor homes full of adventurous kids and patient adults. We usually stayed in campgrounds, but not always. I remember one particular segment of the trip, between two distant western towns, where we literally pulled all the motor homes into a prairie field at nightfall after traveling much of the day. We circled like wagons from the Old West and ventured into a nearby woods with my uncle's pistol just in case we encountered something wild. We gathered materials and built a fire in the center of our RV circle. We cooked dinner over the fire and told stories under a star-filled sky made even more alive with sparks sent skyward by the fire's intense heat and shifting logs.

On another of the trip's adventures, a few of the moms dropped us off with our rafts and river equipment somewhere in Idaho along the Snake River. They drove downriver to a pickup point a day's floating and paddling away. Somehow, somewhere in the rapids rounding one bend in the river, Dad lost his glasses and ended up in the river. Or, maybe he fell in the river and then lost his glasses. Either way, he found himself neck deep in the water next to the raft rounding a bend in the river sans glasses. At that moment, coming into view from around the bend, we saw a massive bull moose standing belly deep in the middle of the river. The big bull interrupted his drink to lift and square his head our direction. We were close enough to fully appreciate his backboard-sized antlers and see the water still dripping from the hairs of his massive chin. As he assessed our threat, his powerful, steady gaze seemed to warn that we should change our trajectory. Trajectory change? No can do. The current was too strong. We were too close. We had no plan, no weapons, and Dad was still in the water. Thankfully, the big bull wasn't the least bit threatened by us. He lumbered slowly to a new, less-traveled section of water and looked curiously back as we passed by in quiet appreciation of God's incredible creative work and our good fortune.

Those memories seem as fresh and vibrant today as when they were formed almost forty years ago. Thanks, Mom and Dad, for investing in some really rich life experiences.

Living on sixteen acres in rural Indiana, go-karts, three-wheelers, dirt bikes, and snowmobiles were all pleasures of my youth, willingly funded by Dad and at least tolerated by Mom. Directly and indirectly, Dad taught me how to drive, respect, and operate machinery. He instructed, monitored, and carefully extended proverbial leash so we could learn by doing and develop our own good judgment.

In the same vein as my prior reflection on motor-homing in the mountains, I vividly recall, as a twelve-year-old boy of barely eighty-five pounds, seeing a frenetic 114 mph tucked behind the bars of a 1981 Yamaha SRX 440 on a lake in Wisconsin. I was able to enjoy this experience not because I was a young professional snowmobiler—and certainly not because my father was foolish or reckless—but because I had experienced many things in my youth, and I was prepared. I had grown in responsibility and expectation, and I had well-formed faculties of judgment for a boy my age. I was a good rider, and Dad had set my bar high. Dad understood my skill set and my level of maturity. He believed both were adequate for this opportunity, and he trusted that I would bring them to bear in a straight line on a barren, frozen lake in Wisconsin: "Focus, enjoy, and don't make your turn until you are almost stopped and know for sure the coast behind you is clear."

Mom and Dad certainly tried to build safety into our activities, but they were far from fanatical about it. We got by with some things that probably should have done us more harm, but, by God's mercy, they didn't. Through the spinouts, wipeouts, rollovers, crashes, and near crashes, we escaped significant injury and learned to do things better each time. We improved, fine-tuned judgment, and reduced risk with each experience. Mom and Dad never lost perspective. Damage to toys could be repaired; damage to kids could not.

Certainly, I recall Dad being upset with crashes and damage, but between kid and machine, we never doubted which was more important. If I've heard him say it once, I've heard him say it a hundred times: "Son, once you think you've got it mastered, you better put it away." Over the years, I've crashed several times and come close to crashing on many other occasions. In almost every case, I did indeed think I had it mastered and should have put it away, but I didn't. Young men full of testosterone and bravado, you in particular need to hear and heed these words. This instruction is so important to you that it warrants repeating.

Once you think you've got it mastered,
you better put it away.

As I got older, I developed a more intense passion for toys, speed, riding, and driving. You name it, I was into it, *really* into it. I subscribed to a multitude of different magazines ranging from *Car and Driver* to *Motocross Action*. I shared Dad's love for Corvettes and was all about snowmobiles, three-wheelers, and dirt bikes. The walls of my room were covered, quite literally, with hundreds, maybe thousands, of pictures and posters of dream machines and ripsnorting action of all sorts.

My brother's first motorcycle was a used Harley-Davidson dirt bike, followed shortly thereafter by a new Kawasaki KE100. Eventually, my good fortune followed with a brand-new 1980 Kawasaki KM100. I was nine years old. I remember being in the showroom, ogling this machine and numerous others. I wanted this machine, but I don't recall having pushed my parents hard for it. Nagging wasn't my way, and it would not have been tolerated anyway. Much to my surprise, a short while later, Mom sat down in my room to tell me they were buying this motorcycle for me. To this day, it still stirs up strong emotions. Certainly, in those first moments, I was happy, but shortly after my surprise, I cried heavy tears. I felt guilty. I wasn't worthy of their spending that kind of money on me. I hadn't done anything beyond verbalizing my admiration over this cool, shiny mechanical thing. Sure, I said I liked and wanted it, but I didn't really want them to have to pay for it. I couldn't take back my words and actions that sent them down this road. Mom listened. She combined her tears of pride with my tears of guilt as she assured me that I was a worthy young man. She calmly explained that our family was doing well financially and that she and Dad wanted me to have this new motorcycle. The kind and caring balm Mom so skillfully applied that day holds prominent place in my memory of the experience.

My friend Pat and I with my KM100, circa 1982

I couldn't believe it. I was a good kid and always tried to do and to be what my parents wanted. Motorcycle or no motorcycle, I loved and respected them just the same. Could I be getting a new motorcycle of my very own? Looking back, this strong desire to love and respect my parents must have risen to a higher level with that experience and their loving generosity. At the time, I attributed the gesture more to Dad than to Mom, probably unfairly. Dad was the primary breadwinner and head of our household, and this was a mechanical, manly thing. I presumed Dad was the instigator, but I also knew Mom was in on it. Dad would never have gone through with such a purchase if Mom were not fully on board. They were a good team that way, loving and respectful of one another.

While the seventies were productive, fun, and certainly formative, the eighties were haymaking years for our family, both literally and figuratively. Literally speaking, much of my summer work from 1984 through the end of the decade consisted of baling hay. Without exaggeration, I put up thousands upon thousands of bales of hay in those years. It was hard, sweaty, lucrative work. I loved it.

The eighties were also great years of growth and progress in Dad's crop-insurance business. Dad was still very present in our lives, but his business was flourishing, and he was capitalizing. Dad was making figurative hay while his sun was shining. Dad was well known and well respected throughout our farming community as the insurance agent of choice. He was one agent folks could count on to be fair and honest and to have their backs should they experience losses on their farms. As a one-man agency, Dad wrote and serviced a staggering number of insurance policies. No agency with fewer than four agents could match his one-man show. One of the insurance products he offered was something called *multiperil crop insurance*, which covered, as the name would suggest, a multitude of risks to which one's crops might be exposed, drought included.

The summer of 1988 quite possibly guaranteed Dad's next decade of solid business. The summer wore on and on with very little rain. There was none in the forecast. The crops showed physical stress, and the farmers showed mental stress from the lack of rain. Many had written policies with my dad early in the season. These farmers were saddened by the lack of rain but remained reasonably peaceful. For others, a day of reckoning was fast approaching, a deadline beyond which they could no longer purchase this insurance.

For several days as the deadline approached, from sunup to sundown, there was some version of a line at the door of my dad's small office in Fowler. At the close of one of those final days, I recall Dad coming home exhausted later in the evening, commenting with frazzled satisfaction that he had written X or Y millions of dollars' worth of insurance that day, his highest ever. He was proud. I was proud of him. We were all proud of him.

Dad's high point wasn't just about the financial windfall. The totality of his reward came in the ensuing months as he worked diligently for his customers, ensuring that the insurance they paid for found its way fairly back to them if rain never came. Rain didn't come, but Dad's coverage did. His customers survived the drought to farm another day.

DAD RECEIVING MORE INSURANCE AWARDS, CIRCA 1990

While Dad was making financial hay, I was baling literal hay, walking bean rows, cutting whiskey barrels for planters at a small-town "factory," and working every extra hour I could for local farmers. Sometimes in the fall, I would get up well before dawn and get in a few hours of field work before school, then several hours after. Following Friday-night football games, I often jumped in the tractor and plowed all night long. When the sun began to illuminate the horizon, I was reawakened and inspired by the vast expanse of rich topsoil that I had turned over the course of the night. It lay black, peaceful, and aromatic in stark contrast to the undisturbed, frost-covered soil yet to be plowed. I watched the fog rise with the sun and the frost disappear. I loved the smell of freshly turned soil and the sound of a pulling diesel, and I longed for the arrival of Elmina, my boss's kindly wife. She would appear on the horizon, timed with the break of dawn, bringing a Mountain Dew, a Snickers bar, a pleasant morning greeting, and a smile.

High school years were wonderful. No drugs, no alcohol, no trouble for me. Basketball, wrestling, and work abounded. I had a treasured steady girlfriend with shared interests and values. I treated her with respect, and I honored her purity as well as my own. I ran with a good crowd of grounded, hardworking country kids who had their heads on mostly straight. We weren't perfect, to be sure, but we were good kids enjoying a great time of life. I had a pretty solid nest egg set aside and an adequate supply of disposable fun money to boot. I was a thriving, happy young man doing my best to follow Dad's example.

My first car was Dad's 1981 Volkswagen Rabbit, a gray five-speed diesel…"chickmobile." He didn't give it to me. I bought it for $1400 cash in 1986. It had roughly a hundred thousand miles on the clock. It was paid for, it was reliable, and it took almost nothing for fuel. Dad let me use diesel from a tank we had at home because it consumed so little. My high school sweetheart was not a material girl, and I was established enough that no one poked fun at me or my car. In the student parking lot of my rural Indiana high school, my VW fit right in. It might have been a hooptie in the eyes of some, but it was my hooptie, and I owned it and cared for it as a proud owner should. It could just as well have been a Corvette. It was mine, outright, with hard-earned, sweat-stained money. One day, it would be a Corvette— multiple Corvettes, actually.

My VW represented a special sort of connection with Dad beyond the fact that he owned it first. For the first five years of its life, it was his work car, the lesser of the two family cars described previously. I vividly recall Dad's simple words as they related to his spartan little Rabbit: "Son, I could drive a Cadillac, but it is not who I am, and it doesn't send the right message to my customers when I drive onto their farms. I'm working for them."

Those brief sentences stuck with me. There is nothing wrong with a Cadillac, a Corvette, a Maserati, or any other nice vehicle for that matter, but our identities are not tied up in our cars and possessions. We don't do what we do, or possess what we possess, for appearances or positive affirmations. We also don't associate to any great degree with people who assign undue importance to "stuff." Mom and Dad taught us to be conservative and humble. We were to appreciate priceless blessings every day and to enjoy rich experiences and possessions that carried price tags only when the conditions were right and when we had the money to pay for them in full.

Enjoy blessings. Avoid materialism.

"For the love of money is the root of all evils."

(I Timothy 6:10)

CHAPTER 3

COLLEGE EDUCATION

Lessons on Teamwork, Good Crowds, Timely
Handshakes, Serving, and Apologizing

IN THE FALL OF 1989, I LEFT FOR COLLEGE. MY OLDER SIBLINGS HAD LEFT home a few years prior. My brother, Shawn, was serving our country in the Air Force, and my sister, Sherry, was pursuing her passion to become a professional hair stylist. My departure for college turned our parents into empty nesters. We loaded the last of the essentials into my Rabbit and our old, ugly, rust-ravaged 1977 Toyota Hilux pickup that Dad had bought from my high school physics teacher and wrestling coach for $350. Once everything was loaded, my parents; my girlfriend, Trina; and I headed south on US 41 toward Terre Haute, home to, among other things, Rose-Hulman Institute of Technology and Indiana State University.

For those unfamiliar, Rose-Hulman is a highly rated private engineering, math, and science school. At the time I attended, it was still all male. Females began to matriculate in 1994. Rose-Hulman attracts some of the world's brightest aspiring engineers. Though I graduated third in my high school class of 170 students, my transcript and test scores were barely adequate for admission to Rose. I had to start two weeks early in a jump-start program to bring my math aptitude up to the point where most freshmen tested in. I enrolled squarely in the bottom ten percent of this freshman class. As one might imagine, since it is a respected private school, Rose is on the expensive side. At the time I attended, tuition was on the order of $13,000 per year. Some thirty years later, in 2021, tuition is roughly $72,000 per year. It was a stretch for our family, but Mom and Dad made sacrifices to ensure the best education was available.

There was little discussion on how college would be funded, though I'm not sure why. It was my intention to pay as much as I could pay, and it was Mom and Dad's intention that I pay none. They expected me to focus entirely on my studies. They were proud, they were prepared, and 100% focus is what they believed would be best. My parents knew, however, the value of hard work and of having skin in the game for something of real value. As a result, I participated in a work-study program to help with tuition. I also worked each summer between sessions, and I paid for one out of every three terms for the first two years of college. There were no loans out of necessity that I can recall, only perhaps a few that provided interest-free or tax-advantaged money that my parents were savvy enough to leverage for a short time.

College years were a blur, and a smaller number of my memories involve Dad, or any family member for that matter. I recall coming home whenever it was feasible to enjoy Mom's home-cooked meals. I remember borrowing Dad's farm truck for various personal and fraternity needs on occasion. I remember breaks between terms and those rare weekends at home, sitting around the kitchen table, catching up on school and life with Mom. Dad and I would catch up, too, in a more concise, factual, "Is there anything you need?" sort of way while we worked on some project or tinkered with something. As it turned out, in the summer between my freshman and sophomore years, there was something I needed. It just took me a while to realize it and ask. The story is a bit peculiar and requires some setting of the stage, but if you will follow its formation, the story does eventually integrate more life lessons from Dad and others.

Rose-Hulman's mascot is an elephant. That's right; she is an elephant affectionately named "Rosie." By some means, a tradition had developed over the years whereby Rosie made a celebration lap around the track encircling the football field each time the Fightin' Engineers scored a touchdown. Rosie was not a real living, breathing pachyderm. Rather, she was a tubular steel structure shaped, wrapped, and adorned to look like an elephant. She was approximately eight feet tall by twelve feet long, and she rolled along on a small four-wheeled wagon frame. When our team put another six points on the scoreboard, a small group of willing freshmen yoked themselves to Rosie's frame just in front of her trunk. At an easy jog, the helpful freshmen towed her around the track as if she were a parade float.

I was one such helpful freshman, perhaps the most willing and the most openly critical of the plodding display. In 1989, I was the one shoehorned inside Rosie's tubular rib cage, assigned with the task of moving her U-jointed head here and there to make her appear more lifelike. While it was a memorable experience, to say the least, I don't recall the whole production being overly impressive, considering Rose-Hulman was widely regarded as the premier undergraduate engineering institution in the country. I believed our aspiring engineers could do better, and I said so. I was given the opportunity to prove it.

My work-study assignment had two parts. One included work in the machine shop under the tutelage of a great mentor named Mike. Mike was a multitalented craftsman, machinist, manager of the machine shop, and creator of Rosie's mechanicals. Being almost nineteen years old, full of gusto and self-supposed wisdom, I shared with Mike my criticisms of the then-current manifestation of Rosie and her tradition. Mike patiently listened with a quiet smile, nodding occasionally. He willingly offered to support my suggestions for change. In Mike, I had my first solid advocate and helper.

The other portion of my work-study assignment was with the Buildings and Grounds Department, led by another solid fellow named Ron. Ron was my second supporter for a Rosie refresh. His support afforded me access to more "tinker items" that proved helpful, as well as access to a small bit of garage space not far from the machine shop where I stored the in-process project. With plenty of help and oversight from Mike, I used the gaps in my work-study time and many hours of personal time over the course of my freshman year to outfit Rosie with propulsion and steering. The new Rosie needed to go, stop, and turn with or without a crew of freshmen.

A forsaken three-horsepower Briggs & Stratton mower engine, a salvage cast-iron flywheel, plenty of chain, a few sprockets, a minuscule transmission that converted vertical drive to horizontal drive, a few pulleys, a belt and engagement device, some ingenuity, and plenty of will allowed Mike and me to mount the engine at Rosie's backside. We ran power down one back leg and exhaust down the other back leg, leaving just enough room in her belly for an operator. Rosie was mobile in two directions: forward and backward.

Now that I'm reflecting in earnest on this project, I'm recalling that Rosie had almost nothing for brakes. Perhaps we used a wedge-shaped block of wood or metal to drag on one of the rear tires like on a discount-store go-kart. I really don't recall; braking wasn't the biggest fish we needed to fry. It was a good thing Rosie was slow and the track around the football field was flat.

More chain, more sprockets, a couple of fabricated shafts and links, a hard bucket seat from McDonald's, some refuse lumber, a steering wheel taken from a lawn mower, a big mirror, more ingenuity and will, and suddenly we had ourselves a removable cockpit and the ability to steer. The final element needed was water. Wouldn't it be cool to shoot water out of Rosie's trunk onto unsuspecting fans and cheerleaders? Yes, it would! Mike worked his magic. A vintage stainless-steel fire extinguisher appeared from Mike's collection of stuff. It just happened to fit nicely within the tubular confines of Rosie's right front leg. Some flexible rubber hose, copper tubing, a few fittings and clamps, a simple mounting-and-coupling system, and the all-important handle with which to "fire" the liquid agitation—finally the mechanical beast was ready for homecoming. Big victory!

Big problem: the mechanicals were completed just before we got out of school for the summer. My buddies and I were busy working internships in other places. Summer was rapidly drawing to a close. Without her "skin" and decorations, no one would recognize the spruced-up pachyderm as our beloved Rosie the elephant. The sights, sounds, and alumni were to converge for the first home game in little more than a month. "Hey, Dad, I think I might need a hand." Dad had no idea what he was in for.

I am neither an artist nor a sculptor. Neither is my dad. However, one fine weekend in August 1990, Dad joined me in the awkwardly creative process of making Rosie look like an elephant. There were sheets and sheets of project foam, cases of spray paint, more foam, quarts of glue, zip ties, wire, a big section of rope for the tail, and plenty of oversight from an uncle who lived in the area. Materials, utilitarian creativity, and hours of quality working time converged to birth something like an elephant from an endoskeleton. By the end of the weekend, we were done, really done. Rosie was ready inside and out. There would be no project handoff, no mascot on hiatus until the second or third home game of the season, and no transfer of concern about completion of the project to others. Tradition was not going to die or be an embarrassment on our watch. Rosie had a new lease on life, and she was ready, thanks to the help, guidance, and participation of several great guys, most notably Dad and Mike. I was responsible, but *we* got the job done.

> Not one among us is self-made. At various
> points in life, we all need a little help.

For Rosie's first performance, Mom and Dad made their way down to the big game—something I think they did only once in four years. At the track's edge, Rosie stood ready. In passing, folks seemed to notice her fresh appearance but little else. The new and improved Rosie was a sleeper.

I highly doubt anyone noticed the absence of Rosie's entourage. Perhaps they were too focused on the action moving closer to the end zone. In relative obscurity, one of my fraternity brothers lifted Rosie's tail, pulled the starter cord, and exhaust began sputtering quietly from beneath her left rear foot. Yes, that's right; the starter cord snatched from Rosie's backside was a comical engineering twist. In the excitement, I slipped away to my cockpit within Rosie's rib cage and settled a bit nervously into position as her diminutive mower engine idled with quiet resolve. Touchdown! The signal came. Go time!

ROSIE AND I, HOMECOMING 1990

I was hidden at the helm, and Rosie was moving publicly under her own power for the first time. Since only a couple of fraternity brothers were jogging along her far side, mostly out of view, folks were unprepared for her performance. There was a mirror mounted on the frame below to help me see. It was between my legs like an inverted periscope. The mirror proved to be entirely useless. I could see almost nothing. Thankfully, top speed was *maybe* 5 mph. To steer, I focused only on the lines of the track beneath me and listened for laughter, cries for redirection, or perhaps cries of pain. Yes, it is true; I did run down one male cheerleader in that first thirty yards, but he quickly rebounded. Rosie's trunk must have taken him out. Once he fell, I did see his shoes and legs coming into my path, but he managed to scramble up and away with mere moments to spare. Hilarious tragedy averted. My nervous anticipation gave way to rejoicing as arcs of water, invisible to me, fanned over the multitudes. There were cheers from the crowd and unmistakable laughter from my fraternity brothers. I saw only lines on the track, a few lower legs and shoes of those who dared approach, and fresh water showered from Rosie's trunk in the moments prior. I was delighted.

I couldn't see him, but I'm sure Dad was sharing in my amusement and pride. One year prior, I had opened my mouth and boldly proclaimed that a bunch of aspiring engineers could do better than a lifeless mascot toted along by a team of plodding freshmen. With the help of several quality men and a handful of zealous young engineers, we did. Sometimes it is best to take action, to do something, even if it is wrong, rather than to coexist with convention and mediocrity. Just be sure you have the requisite gumption, the grit, and a team of helpers to see it through to a proper finish, in this case, the literal end zone.

There's no way around this truth. Rose-Hulman was tough. Academic success for me came at a price. Almost every day—and Sundays were no exception—included six to eight hours of homework, lab work, and study on top of whatever time was spent in the lab or classroom. I was involved in campus ministry, joined a reputable fraternity, worked hard, and kept my nose clean. Catholicism became both more personal and more important to me than it had been during youth and adolescence. I had as much fun as the intensity of the work allowed. Work first; play later. Dad drilled this order into us early. I thrived on such challenges of college and performed well academically in spite of the rigor—perhaps because of the rigor. Growing into a better, stronger, more independent young man, I developed healthy bonds and positive associations with other solid young men on a common journey.

In the second or third quarter of our freshman year, I learned of a very lucrative scholarship awarded by General Motors to just a few students near the end of their sophomore year. I was immediately drawn to the challenge, to the opportunities with GM, and to the many financial benefits my family would receive should I be fortunate enough to win one of the coveted scholarships. As luck and good crowds would have it, one scholarship recipient from each of the two previous years was a fraternity brother of mine: Paul and Ryan. Their guidance, encouragement, and mentorship were greatly appreciated and certainly helpful in my scholarship quest.

SIDEBAR 4:
POSITIVE ASSOCIATIONS

Perhaps this is a good place to divert onto a short, related tangent regarding the importance of running with the right crowd. We've probably all heard sayings such as "If you run with dogs, eventually you'll end up with fleas," or "If you hang out with bank robbers, someday you'll find yourself driving the getaway car." Solomon's wisdom, poured out in the book of Proverbs, clearly illustrates similar points throughout, but with particular poignancy in these verses: "Walk with wise men and you will become wise, but the companion of fools will fare badly" (Proverbs 13:20) and "As iron sharpens iron, so man sharpens his fellow man" (Proverbs 27:17).

I ran with a great group of men in college. My fraternity was chosen thoughtfully, and my closest associations were developed carefully. I chose the Pi Kappa Alpha national fraternity, whose preamble reads, "For the establishment of friendship on a firmer and more lasting basis; for the promotion of brotherly love and kind feeling; for the mutual benefit and advancement of the interests of those with whom we sympathize and deem worthy of our regard; we have resolved to form a fraternity, believing that thus we can most successfully accomplish our object." Our particular chapter's founding at Rose-Hulman centered on the emphasis of academics and the de-emphasis of alcohol. We were jokingly referred to by the other fraternities on campus as "The Milk-and-Cookie Boys," and we proudly embraced our title.

Our fraternity held a higher grade point average than any other fraternity on campus and a higher GPA than the all-student average of the whole school every quarter of every year I attended. Is it any wonder that I was able to leverage the experience of GM-scholarship recipients from two previous years right there among the ranks of my fraternity brothers?

Some may cling to stories and images of idiocy and tomfoolery from fraternities and sororities, much of which does exist, but this doesn't exist everywhere. Fraternity life cannot be painted with such a broad brush. Approached carelessly, Greek life in college can bring real problems. Vet carefully and invest wisely, however, and it can foster life lessons of great value and forge friendships of great prize. Paul, Ryan, Ken, Todd, Sean, Bill, Irv, Clay, Jason, and many more, thank you for some great years and for your continued friendship.

Run with the right crowd or you may find yourself crippled. Associations are important.

Back to my scholarship quest, in order to be considered for the GM scholarship, it was critical to maintain the highest possible academic performance in the most challenging, most applicable classes. It was important to involve oneself in honorable and contributory extracurricular and community activities. It was important to develop marketable mechanical skills and knowledge. All of this was clear. It was also clear that, should I get a shot at this scholarship, I would have to bring passion and my sharpest A game to the written application and the interview.

I set my sights on this scholarship, and my shot came. I was one of five sophomores selected to compete for a single scholarship offered to mechanical-engineering students. A second GM scholarship was made available to a different group of electrical-engineering students. In my group of mechanical engineers, three of the five students selected carried straight 4.0 GPAs. One, named Mark, carried a straight 4.0 with a double major: mechanical engineering and mathematics. My piddly 3.9, in mechanical engineering only, made me a clear underdog, at least on paper.

Delco Remy, one of GM's in-house suppliers of starters, alternators, and related control systems, was the sponsoring division. By this, I mean they were the division that was going to pay 100% of the bill for the winner's junior and senior academic years. Delco Remy was going to provide summer internships between academic years, and they would most certainly be interested in capitalizing on their investment by employing the award recipient after graduation.

This scholarship was a big deal, a huge deal. In 1990 dollars, receiving this scholarship was worth at least $40,000 directly, and the substance it added to the winner's résumé is difficult to quantify. In 2021, if this same scholarship is still awarded, it wouldn't miss a total direct value of $200,000 by much. Mom and Dad knew of the scholarship and the stakes. They knew to pray and support but not to impose or to pressure. I knew they were in my corner, no matter what.

With the help of my mentors, I prepared as if my life depended on it. I felt as though my academic life did. I recall researching a great deal about GM, and Delco Remy in particular. I recall making numerous copies of each and every application page and handling and protecting the original pages with great care. In those days, there was no Internet. Applicants didn't fill out a perfectly formatted form online at a secure website with a username and password. There was no going back for a redo, and there was no "save and exit" for later. Applicants were given *one* physical application form. That was it. It was to be completed in ink. It could be handwritten, typed, or printed by a properly formatted printer. Once completed, it was to be returned by physical mail days before the interview. This application was no place for sloth or inattention to any detail.

I reasoned and articulated my responses carefully and improved them again and again with the counsel of many. Word documents were formatted for each page with the exact position, spacing, and font size that fit optimally and printed with the best, cleanest laser printer to be found on campus. The printed text and handwritten elements had to look as sharp as possible on the original application. I practiced signing my name over and over and over again with the best black pens available and must have gone through at least ten application copies, complete with signature pages, before feeding the originals into the printer or exposing them to my pen. There were even multiple iterations to improve the printing on the mailing envelope. Yes, the details were *that* important, at least in my mind. Once printed and signed, my application was indeed the absolute best that I could make it given the time available. With application signed, sealed, and delivered, it was on to the interview.

Interviewing well comes down to quickly developing a relationship of trust, conveying authenticity, and carefully steering the interview toward your strengths and desires and away from your weaker areas where possible. Engaging, relatable life experiences and illustrations can be very helpful in building trust and communicating sincerity. By contrast, the inability to build trust, the inability to steer the conversation, the inability to relate on a practical level, and the inability to express your desires tactfully can be interview killers. Back then, I knew these things to be true but didn't understand the depth of these truths as I do today. I just did the best I could based on how I had been raised and the examples I had seen growing up. All of the grammar, manners, professionalism, and respect in dealing with others that I had been taught directly and indirectly by my parents, teachers, coaches, bosses, fraternity brothers, and others proved useful in this most important interview.

Never be late. Better to be an hour
early than a single minute late.

I've heard the great Jerry Rice talk about similarly stern punctuality directives handed down from his father. Insistence on punctuality from a demanding father kept Jerry Rice from ever being late to anything—practices, games, interviews, or sponsor commitments—throughout his entire illustrious football career.

Punctuality reflects your values. You will never
be late for something you cherish.

I showed up to my interview with plenty of time to spare. I looked professional. I felt mentally prepared, confident, and strong. I was clean-shaven, well groomed, and well dressed. I had long ago been thinking of questions interviewers might ask and responses I might provide. I had relatable life experiences adaptable to a multitude of possible questions. I had materials to take notes, a few notecards of information about GM and Delco Remy that might come in handy, and a series of questions of my own should the opportunity to ask present itself. Finally, I had a copy of my written application so that I had the exact answers I had written previously. I was ready.

My interview was scheduled for thirty minutes. The candidate just before me emerged about five minutes before my interview was to start. He was a good guy. We exchanged a few thoughts about how his interview had gone and wished each other good luck, and I did my best to center myself and focus in those few moments before the door was opened to me. I breathed deeply, offered a few words of thanks and gratitude to my Creator, and asked for His guiding hand over the experience and my performance.

The communication and value of a proper handshake cannot
be overstated. Never give a limp fish, and always restrain your
grip as needed for those with smaller or more delicate hands.

Dad has always had big, sturdy hands like in the 1991 Holly Dunn country song "Daddy's Hands." They were strengthened and hardened by work. They were etched and scarred by life. Dad's handshake was firm, controlled, and welcoming. It is a good handshake yet today. Dad and other men taught me to look another in the eye and shake hands in a positive, deliberate way without backing down or attempting to overpower, neither cutting the connection short nor overstaying my welcome. I always aspired to shake hands like Dad. In my days of meeting folks and selecting a fraternity, I was told on occasion that my handshake alone would get me a job. I hoped such was the case for this scholarship, as well.

I was welcomed into the interview room and given the opportunity to shake hands with each of three interviewers. After exchanging a few opening pleasantries, the interviewers sat and invited me to do the same. I settled into my seat and then into my groove with the first few questions. In short order, with my full support, the conversation turned sharply toward my activities outside the classroom. The interviewers expressed particular interest in Rosie and her rebirth. This was a welcome turn and topic. I quickly reached a level of respectful comfort with each of these seasoned engineers. In what seemed like no time, we were talking and sketching illustrations on my notepad about how this design was developed or about how that challenge was addressed. The conversation ventured into work experiences on the farm growing up, cars and trucks I was into, and some of the latest things Delco Remy was working on where perhaps I could learn and be of some assistance.

The interview was comfortable, natural, and well balanced. It went beautifully. Before any of us knew it, regrettably, it was time to stop talking and wrap it up. We were out of time, perhaps even a little late. The next candidate was waiting outside. It was Mark. The interviewers and I shared another round of appreciative, respectful handshakes and closing remarks. They bid me farewell and good luck. I couldn't have scripted a better interview.

As I walked out of the room, and the door shut behind me for the interviewers to collect their thoughts, I breathed a grateful sigh, thanked God privately, and smiled contentedly. Mark was waiting. I shared a few insights and well-wishes with him. My relief and optimism exiting the interview room might have been a little unsettling for Mark in spite of his academic credentials. The interviewers and I used all of my allotted time, plus some, and I walked out with a cautiously confident air. Mark didn't appear to be a hands-on engineer, and I'm pretty sure he didn't come from a rural background that afforded him the sorts of practical mentorship and experience that I was blessed to receive from my dad and various employers. Mark's academic strengths were clear, but it would be difficult to predict how any experiential voids might sit with the interviewers.

I sat down again in the waiting area to make my own summary notes as Mark got started with his interview. I wanted to capture the highlights correctly so that when I went to write my forthcoming thank-you notes, I could make the notes appropriately personal, and the passage of time wouldn't confound my memory. As I drew my notes to a close and was packing my things to leave for the next class, Mark emerged from the interview room, barely ten minutes after he had entered. Astonished, I swallowed under my breath, "What gives?" Naturally, without presumption, I asked him how his interview had gone. He shared that he didn't think it had gone very well. Mark really wanted to work for a different division of General Motors, Allison Gas Turbine, not Delco Remy. Apparently, he had informed the interviewers of his interest in Allison without adequately connecting the dots on how he could first contribute to Delco Remy and their business—bad move.

Be careful. Be observant. Think before you act or speak.

His interviewers had sensed the second-tier position they held in Mark's career plan, and they had no interest in investing in him. From my vantage point, the strongest academic candidate had just thrown away his opportunity at this scholarship, leaving a field of only four. At nearly every turn, wisdom—the fruit of the academics of life—trumps education drawn merely from the printed page. Smart as he was, Mark had thrown this one away.

A short time after the interviews concluded, perhaps only a few hours, my fraternity brother and scholarship mentor, Ryan, who had received this scholarship one year earlier, was waiting expectantly for me outside my classroom as the bell rang. There, in the hall, he shook my hand properly in joyful congratulations. I won! What a memorable way to pass along the news! He didn't have to take time out of his busy schedule to monitor the news. He didn't have to research my schedule and seek me out at the precise moment to be the first to deliver the wonderful announcement. He didn't even have to help me in the first place. But, he did those things. Thank you, Ryan! All of your help, and that gesture in particular, meant a great deal to me.

> Never underestimate the value of service,
> kindness, and consideration to others.

I could barely contain myself on the call home from the payphone in the dorm. "I got it!" I sputtered out to Mom without even saying, "Hello." The relief, joy, and emotions flowed. I couldn't believe my good fortune. I was flying high. I was a GM man, and we were *done* paying for college!

Those moments of joy and celebration were memorable, of course, but it was the weekend that followed that brings this story squarely back to Dad. My parents and I made a plan to meet for dinner to celebrate the scholarship at the famous Beef House Restaurant halfway between home and school. Dad was so pleased with the whole thing that he had spent days prior cleaning out and detailing his latest work car, now a 1986 VW Golf diesel, with the intention of trading me keys at the end of our meal. He was planning to head happily back home with his original 1981 VW Rabbit as I returned to school with his much nicer, newer Golf.

It was a wonderful gesture and would have been a generous gift, but it wasn't meant to be. Mom and Dad listened to my reasoning and respected my decision to pass on their gift. The scholarship was a blessing, something of which to be very proud. We all were excited and proud. Dad's car, however, was his car, not mine. I hadn't worked for his car. I hadn't paid for his car, and he and Mom had already spent thousands on getting me this far in school. I felt that it was a great time for me to *start paying them back* where I could, not to receive more good fortune. I greatly appreciated the thought and the gesture, but I could not accept it. Aside from the financial aspect, which was not comfortable for me, Dad's car was a Volkswagen, and I would soon be funded and groomed by General Motors. My VW would send the wrong message to GM as I drove onto their proverbial "farms." After dinner, we returned to our own places with our own cars, full of good food, goodwill, happiness, and hope.

SIDEBAR 5:

GRATITUDE AND SORROW

While this entire collection of thoughts fits neatly under the umbrella of gratitude, it is worth taking a few extra moments to elaborate on the importance of gratitude. Gratitude is among the healthiest of human emotions and conditions of the heart. Expressing gratitude does wonders both for the deliverer and for the recipient. Communicating gratitude effectively is becoming a lost art ripe for rediscovery. Almost nothing is more beneficial to everyone involved than the sharing of genuine, sincere thanks. The value packed into a slightly prolonged handshake, meaningful eye-to-eye contact, and a well-timed, thankful smile is almost immeasurable. Of similar value is a well-crafted, handwritten thank-you note sent by way of old-fashioned mail. Almost everyone enjoys receiving things of value in the mail, especially personally addressed, heartfelt appreciation. Traditional thank-you notes are a must, particularly when, for whatever reason, face-to-face gratitude is difficult or impossible to offer.

My mother taught—rather, she *insisted*—that we write quality thank-you notes for many things almost immediately following the gift or the gesture. Even if the note traveled only a short distance to a nearby friend or neighbor, it had to be written and sent just the same. Thank-you notes are not just boxes that must be checked after opening one's wedding gifts. I have never forsaken Mom's practice of writing thank-you notes. It has served me well, and it serves our children well today as we insist on the same practice. You can be sure that each of my Delco Remy interviewers personally received a proper, handwritten thank-you note following my interview. It was important that I thank them for their time, for their consideration, and for the opportunity to compete for the coveted scholarship, whether or not I was fortunate enough to win. Gratitude smooths the bumps in life's journey and fosters a spirit of goodwill. Don't underestimate the benefits of a grateful, appreciative spirit.

On the opposite end of the human emotion spectrum is another very powerful emotion I would be remiss not to mention: sorrow. Perhaps men need to hear this most of all, including me. If you have said or done something wrong, swallow your pride, own up to whatever your portion of the wrong might be, state your sorrow for the offense sincerely and completely, and do all you can not to repeat the offense. Doing so works wonders. We all mess up from time to time. To withhold apology is both cowardly and unproductive. When needed, apologize and move forward with love and better intentions. With time, after you have apologized correctly, the damaged relationship may recover to a new and stronger position of gratitude and appreciation for both parties.

Apologize sincerely. Don't repeat the wrong.

I reflect with some regret on one particular example from my college days when I did not handle a conflict with one of my good friends correctly. I compounded the problem by failing to offer a prompt, sincere apology that was fitting to the situation. Time has clouded some of the details, but I recall having been the ringleader in organizing attendees for a country-music concert that was coming to town. I purchased and paid for a sizeable group of tickets well in advance of the concert. Quite a number of our group were planning to attend. I needed certainty in their decisions to attend, and I asked that each person reimburse me promptly in order to offset my initial cash outlay. I became increasingly annoyed when this particular fraternity brother waffled on his decision to attend and further delayed his reimbursement once he decided to go. I indirectly asked for him to step up with his decision and his money on a number of occasions. Nothing got him moving, and I was frustrated. Since we had a large number in our group, seating was broken into two different sections. I decided that since he had left me hanging for so long, I was under no obligation to ensure he had priority seating. That was a poor way to handle my frustration. Confronting the matter early and clearly, resolving it properly, then expressing gratitude for understanding and compliance would have transformed the entire situation. Hindsight is always twenty-twenty. Irv, you didn't deserve the careless treatment I provided in that experience. I would never handle a situation in that way again. I am sorry. Please forgive me, Brother.

CHAPTER 4

GM AND LEADERSHIP

Lessons on Generosity, Listening Well, Sorry
Purchases, and the Value of Your Word

THE SUMMER OF 1991, MY FIRST WITH GENERAL MOTORS, WAS FANTASTIC.
I don't remember exactly when or exactly how I met my GM mentor, Ken,
but I do remember converging on our common interests within moments
of introduction. Ken and I hit it off immediately. At that time, Ken was a
senior-level management engineer with Delco Remy in Anderson, Indiana.
He is full of life and loves all things fast, most notably Corvettes and
snowmobiles. Ken is a friendly, gregarious man, small in physical stature
but large in personal influence. In my experience, he never belittled,
confined, or discouraged anyone at any time. He's the sort of guy who
would let a foolish comment or ignorant question pass silently by. When
you are with Ken, you know you can do it, whatever "it" may be. You
feel confident and capable; the spring in your step has more bounce just
being around him. Ken is everyone's champion, always positive, always
encouraging, and he has enough personal confidence and capability that
he is always happy to share with others. And, share he does.

Ken was high enough on the GM food chain that he received a
new Corvette to drive as his company car every year. That's right, a
new Vette every year. In the summer of '91, his steed was a steel-gray
six-speed convertible with a black soft-top. In July, as Ken and I were

55

talking about cars, about my search for a GM truck to replace my VW, and about how my summer project was progressing, Ken suggested that we trade cars for the weekend. I silently reacted, *Could you repeat that, please?* Was I, a lowly twenty-year-old intern Ken had known for barely two months, just offered the opportunity to enjoy an entire weekend in Ken's brand-new convertible Corvette while he, a senior GM exec, puttered off in my ten-year-old VW Rabbit diesel? Had I heard Ken correctly? Yes, I had!

KEN'S VETTE AND I, 1991

As graciously and as appreciatively as I could, I took Ken up on his generous offer and enjoyed that Vette perhaps more than I should have. I wasn't abusive or disrespectful, but I did enjoy that Vette. I shared the experience with friends and family, too, especially Dad. Dad and I enjoyed every moment we could with that car—cleaning, pampering, gawking, and certainly driving. Dad, Ken, and I developed a deeper connection that weekend, not with words but with actions and gestures. It would be another six months before Dad and Ken would meet for the first time, but I'm certain they knew and respected each other at some level long before that first meeting.

Ken knows and cares about things below the surface. Ken knew full well that his car would be exercised and enjoyed that weekend. He knew it would be an unforgettable experience and that Dad would most certainly be involved. He also must have had some level of trust that I would use good judgment and return it to him in a condition that was as good as, or better than, when I drove off with it. I'd be willing to bet that Ken knew Dad had trained us that way and that I would stick to my training just as the proverb states.

Dave Ramsey, financial steward, teacher, and popular radio personality, encourages such generosity: "The most fun you will ever have with money is giving it away." That wonderful Corvette wasn't made of gold or physical currency, but Ken's handing me its keys was heartfelt generosity just the same. That's how a senior executive at GM smiles leaving the parking lot on a Friday afternoon in a ten-year-old VW Rabbit diesel sporting a whole fifty-two horsepower. Thank you, Ken!

Joy is spelled one way:
Jesus, others, yourself—in that order.

Though I desperately wanted to fly the right flag and drive the right GM vehicle that first summer, it had to wait. I did not find what I was looking for in the used market, and I was in no position to buy the brand-new S-10 pickup I visited repeatedly that summer in the dealership. Sure, I could have borrowed money, but my parents' response was cold any time the topic came up. My old VW was getting me by, the used market was thin, it certainly wasn't the right time for a brand-new vehicle, and my GM bosses and friends knew my heart. My day for GM ownership was coming but had not yet arrived. "Patience is a virtue," Mom would always say, much to my displeasure.

Sometime in the fall of 1992, early in my junior year, as I was walking back to the dorm from one of my last classes of the day, I saw my parents seated on a bench near the path to my dorm. I wasn't expecting them. They had something they wanted to show me. Dad had found and bought a beautiful 1984 Chevy C-10 pickup in hopes that I would like it and that it would check my GM-vehicle box. I did like it, a lot. Dad made a great, instinctive call. I ended up owning that truck for nearly ten years.

It wasn't a gift; we had already covered that. Rather, it was Dad acting on a hunch with proper timing and disposable cash. The Chevy was about $3500, and Dad was my bank. He took payments with no interest as regularly as I was able to make them over the following summer until my loan was paid off. Within a matter of weeks, with a heavy heart and plenty of fond memories, I sold my old VW Rabbit to an eager fraternity brother for $1400, the same amount I had paid for it more than six years and forty thousand miles earlier. The cash went straight to my loan with Dad. I was finally "properly dressed" for work at GM, and I had a nice, responsible used Chevy truck with a small loan to Dad, not to the bank. I was really proud of my truck. Good call, Dad.

The early 1990s seemed to fly by. I was thankful to be close enough during college to slip home on occasional weekends and at breaks between quarters to stay connected with my family. While I was wrapped up in academics and job pursuits, Dad was busy running with his victories in crop-insurance circles. His work ethic, his service to others, his good name, and the value of his word fueled impressive growth in his business. He and Mom were routinely wined and dined at annual conventions where top offices and agents were recognized. San Francisco, New Orleans, San Diego, Tucson, and Hawaii several times—every year brought some new reward and celebration of Dad's high achievement. His was usually one of the top five agencies in the country and the only one with just one agent. Though I had been fortunate to be able to attend one such convention in Acapulco during my senior year of high school, Dad reached his apex later when I was in college and unable to attend. Dad wrote so many millions of dollars' worth of insurance policies that, except for me, *the whole family* was treated to the best Hawaii had to offer, all on the insurance company's tab as a thank-you for Dad's hard work. Even my grandma, Dad's mother-in-law, got to go. Dad was flying on his own high. We were all very proud of him.

Back to Ken, my boss and friend. Ken was the reason my second summer internship at GM happened at the GM proving ground in Milford, MI. Ken listened carefully. He championed my interests and had the power to make things happen. Ken and his team hooked me and another scholarship recipient, Ruben, up with an apartment and basic furnishings in Ann Arbor, Michigan, along with coveted summer work assignments at the proving ground. Ruben didn't have a car, so my Chevy and I provided his shuttle service during another great GM summer experience. With this experience, my appetite was truly whetted for the proving-ground environment and for hands-on motorsports engineering. It is an understatement to say that I was both appreciative and excited going into my senior year.

Before leaving Ken for a short period, it is worth mentioning that my senior year was pleasantly punctuated by another unsolicited loan of Ken's latest Corvette, this time for an entire week. Oh, the fond memories I could share from that week! It's fodder for another discussion, but suffice it to say that I enjoyed this '93 coupe just as much as the '91 convertible.

Corvettes hold a special place in my heart for good reason. Here's how my week with the '93 came to be. While catching up with Ken by phone and providing an update on school, I mentioned that I was looking forward to an upcoming fraternity dance in Cincinnati. Listening attentively, Ken kindly responded, "Well, I'm out of town that week, and my Vette will just be sitting in a secure parking lot at the airport, if you would like to use it." Ken was listening carefully, not for himself and not to prepare his response. No, Ken was listening carefully and thinking generously because that's what he does. It's who he is.

Would I like to use another new Corvette for a week at college with my buddies, culminating in travel with my date to and from a fraternity dance in Cincinnati? Hmm, let's see—yes! I quickly packaged this response into more professional and appreciative words, which I restrained only as long as my excitement would allow. We agreed upon a few logistic details, and I thanked him profusely for another wonderful experience in the making. "I'll leave a note with the keys so the security folks will let you have it. Have fun." What a guy!

Reflecting on this experience, typing these lines, and reading them back to myself gives me pause to consider how I can improve in this area. Do I *really listen* to the speaker in order to understand him where he is—as Ken did with me—or do I listen only for triggers I will use in my response? Am I really that generous, trusting, and replete with goodwill, or do I just like to think that I would be this way in the same circumstances? I'm not sure I can hold my head so high or answer these questions so positively.

Thank you for solid lessons, Ken. Dale Carnegie would be nodding in affirmation. I shall double down on my efforts. I can do better, and I have you to thank for the examples.

DAD AND I, GRADUATION DAY FROM ROSE-HULMAN, 1993

In the spring of 1993, I finally graduated from Rose with high honors, an accomplishment for which I had worked long and hard. Dad was there sharing my joy and relief. Mom, unfortunately, had become very ill that weekend and was not able to attend. Graduation from Rose wasn't the end of my formal education, however. Since I figured it would be prudent to get an advanced degree at some point in life, and I hadn't yet located the role at GM to which I was best suited, I decided to maintain my academic momentum. I tactfully declined GM's open offers in hopes that new offers might be available a short time later, after grad school, if I was careful not to burn precious bridges. Ken was right there supporting my decision, supporting me every step of the way, even ensuring that I had yet another summer internship with GM between undergrad and graduate school if I wanted it. I did. If you didn't already have positive vibes for GM, I hope my reflections might incline your thinking in that direction. I am immensely grateful to GM and certainly to my good friend Ken.

Toward the end of the summer of 1993, my love of Corvettes, my confidence that I would soon be making plenty of money, and my relatively robust bank account from all those years of sweaty farm work, lucrative GM summer internships, and relatively few college bills cast broad, dark shadows over my reasoning. I bought my first Corvette, a red-on-red 1968 427 Tri-Power convertible with a four-speed stick. I just wanted it, and I had the money to buy it. Though Dad loved Corvettes, and still does, I'm not sure how much he liked the idea of storing my car in his garage for the next 6½ years, but he patiently agreed. Now, years later, as a father myself, I understand what Dad already knew: sometimes you just go along and let questionable decisions run their course. Father Time can also be a good teacher.

In the fall of 1993, I matriculated into graduate school at Clemson University in South Carolina. Mom and Dad helped me move, again. This time, I had a real truck and no girlfriend. My time in graduate school proved to be shorter academically but was not without rich lessons and teachable moments from many, Dad and Ken included.

Before accepting Clemson's offer to join their Environmental Systems Engineering (ESE) graduate program, I was surprised to learn that universities often *actually pay you* a small stipend to pursue an advanced degree and complete your research in their program. My stipend wasn't much, but it was enough, and I started out being careful with money as had been my instruction.

Amid research and classwork, I got involved in church and numerous extracurricular activities, including a part-time job helping at a local body shop. I wanted to learn professional painting and bodywork to complement the handyman version learned at home from Dad and Shawn. Yearning to have a project car and a VW diesel again, I netted an ugly, faded 1982 Jetta diesel five-speed with standing water in the footwells of the back seat for $450. This VW became my first real body and paint project. I also reasoned that it would save lots of money on fuel. Stipend and job money slowly started to accumulate in spite of my project.

Once again, I became slightly inebriated by a meager but steady cash flow, youthful confidence, and endless optimism. This concoction enabled a really sorry vehicle purchase. At the time, I didn't think it was so foolish, but it was. What I did *not* need at that time was a rattletrap burnt orange 1966 Chevy pickup truck with mag wheels, a raucous 350 V8, and a three-speed on the tree, but that's what I bought for $1200. For whatever reason, my friends affectionately named the old boy "Clyde." Reminder to self and selected readers:

> The fact that something is cheap doesn't
> necessarily make it a good deal.

I found myself with three vehicles in the parking lot of my apartment complex: the VW project car and two Chevy trucks. Three was too many. I should never have bought the '66 Chevy, at least not at that time. The truck needed too much that I wasn't able to give while immersed in graduate studies and having little income, no house, and no garage. Though foolish economically, the sorry purchase of the '66 did prove to be quite valuable in terms of additional time with Dad and more instruction by example.

Once I came to my senses, I was compelled to sell the '66 Chevy, fast. I knew I needed to recoup as much money as I could, as quickly as I could, even if it meant some amount of financial loss and consumption of humble pie. The truck was physically located in Clemson, South Carolina, but I advertised *both* in South Carolina and near our home in Indiana. At that time, print ads such as newspaper classifieds and regional trader papers were the primary pathways to sell a vehicle. The Internet was in its infancy as far as the public was concerned, and tools such as Craigslist did not exist. As luck would have it, another young man from where I grew up wanted the truck badly and was willing to pay full price. By his interest, his willingness to put down a cash deposit, and his commitment to pay full price, he had done his part. The ball was now in my court to figure out how to get the truck from Clemson, South Carolina, back to Fowler, Indiana—roughly six hundred forty miles away—in a timely fashion.

Driving the truck wasn't a good option for at least two reasons. First, the truck was not in good shape mechanically and would have been at great risk of breaking down and leaving me stranded somewhere in Kentucky with towing and repair bills. Second, once back in Indiana, I would have to get an expensive plane ticket for return to South Carolina, thereby making the truck sale an even bigger financial loss. My second option was to use my 1984 Chevy to tow the truck home on a tow dolly. This was a reasonable idea with one significant hurdle: I didn't have a tow dolly. I borrowed a couple of different tow dollies and tried to rent some, as well, but nothing was wide enough to accommodate the width of this old truck. I gave it a Boy Scout try and came up short. I was ready to throw in the towel, ring the bell, and tell this young man that it wasn't going to happen. After all, he hadn't *actually* put down any money yet, and it just wasn't practical to get the truck back to Indiana. It was my mistake. I should never have advertised back home in the first place.

Throwing the towel into this particular ring, at this particular time, with no more effort than a few failed tow-dolly attempts was not acceptable to Dad. We had given our word, the word of a Geswein, to another member of our local community that we would sell him this truck. That's what we said we were going to do, and we had not yet explored all reasonable options. Dad had both a broader perspective and a bigger tow dolly. Dad carefully measured his dolly in Indiana, and I carefully measured the old truck in South Carolina. It should fit, barely. A glimmer of hope pierced my mental fog, and pieces of the puzzle began coming together. At one of the holiday breaks, I hitched a ride with a friend back to Indiana. At the end of the break, Dad and I hooked his king-size tow dolly up to our old farm truck with plans for southern travel. Our truck at the time was a no-frills, solid, reliable old 1976 GMC Heavy Half, by no means an interstate cruiser.

We bobbed and weaved and bounced our way back to Clemson. The trip was spartan but rewarding. There was conversation, but nothing of great depth or weight that I can recall. It was just Dad and I logging miles—six hundred forty-five of them, to be exact—enjoying each other's company and the unspoken awareness that we were doing the right thing. We rolled into Clemson at dusk, feeling accomplished but tuckered from twelve hours in the old farm truck. We made the short trip to Papa John's for a quick pizza before loading up for the next day's return. There in the parking lot of my apartment complex under the marginal glow of lot lights, we loaded the '66 Chevy onto the dolly, strapped it down, and called it a night. There was little downtime. Dad's departure came early.

MY '66 CHEVY, "CLYDE," AND I, 1994

I'm certain Dad was tired. On day one, there was no load, and I could share the driving duties. On day two, he was pulling an additional 5500 pounds north into the mountains, and there was no one to help drive. This was more like a fourteen-hour trip. I remember feeling guilty that Dad had to crank out another tough day on the road just so I could save face, recoup some money, and honor my word. There was no complaining and no deep discussion about it. There was nothing to discuss. There was no other way. There was one right way, one right thing to do, and this was it. We needed to get busy and get it done. No need for discussion, just get the job done. He was right, again. I learned, again. Dad's lesson:

A man is only as valuable as his word;
honor and protect it at all costs.

Dad delivered the truck that next day to a happy young man who knew little of the story and nothing of the lesson. He simply appreciated the arrival of his truck and knew the name of the family that had sold and delivered it to him. The name *Geswein* was safe in our hometown. The name *Geswein* could resonate only positively for this young man. Dad left no other option.

CHAPTER 5

CLEMSON, ENDURANCE, AND HEART TRUTH

Lessons on Fitting In, Networking, Mr. Ghosn,
Tasmanian Confidence, and Finishing Well

I ENJOYED CLEMSON, BUT I LOATHED MY FIELD OF STUDY, ENVIRONMENTAL Systems Engineering (ESE). The people were fine, the work was necessary, and the intentions were noble, but I did not enjoy the work, not even a little. Don't get me wrong; I am a nature-loving guy and am bent toward protecting, conserving, enjoying, and leaving things better than I found them for the next generation. In this environment, however, I felt like a square peg shredding at my edges and ripping at my flair to fit into an academic and cultural round hole in which I did not belong. I was miserable. When you don't fit in, you are unsettled at your core, and you just want to be somewhere else. I wanted to be somewhere else, but I had to finish what I had started. Quitting was not an option.

As part of God's mysterious plan, the research phase of my graduate work occurred "somewhere else," both literally and figuratively, at Michelin's US2 semifinished-products plant in Sandy Springs, South Carolina. For years, Michelin and Clemson had been attempting to connect and work together on graduate research projects. Mine was the first to actually come to fruition.

My research advisor at Clemson, Dr. White, was more of an agricultural professor and less of an academic. It was a good match. I got him and he got me. We didn't become particularly close, but we understood one another. My project manager at Michelin, Mary Lou, was a wonderful, no-nonsense woman worthy of both respect and friendship. I fondly recall Mary Lou's kindness, her on-point mentorship, and her deep understanding of both chemistry and her department. Finally, I remember being impressed by her absolute command of the French language. I enjoyed working for her, and I learned a great deal.

My research had two distinct phases. The first phase was a prerequisite to the second. In the first phase, I was to clearly identify and quantify each of the waste streams through which certain metals left the facility. It was no small task; US2 is a vast facility producing a wide range of unique products. Once all metal-bearing waste streams were accurately assessed and quantified, I was to present my findings to management, and they would agree on which waste stream(s) to tackle. In this second phase, the tackling phase, I was to research options for minimizing metal waste and determine the feasibility of recovering one particular metal from the largest contributing stream(s).

In autumn 1994, the first phase of my project was drawing to a close, at which point I was to present my initial findings to management. Mary Lou seized upon an opportunity to share these early findings and celebrate the project's successes up to that point with upper-level management from Michelin corporate. Mary Lou's proactivity was far more important than I realized at the time.

She invited me to sit in on a conference where Carlos Ghosn, then CEO of Michelin North America, was in attendance with his aides and management entourage. They traveled in to receive status updates on production, efficiency, safety, and major capital projects at the plant. My small but visible academic research project somehow captured a slot on the agenda. Mary Lou presented. I was there to support silently unless called upon. Mary Lou was kind and proper in her descriptions of the project and of my contributions. I was appreciative for the inclusion and her acknowledgement. More than anything else, I recall being thoroughly impressed by how intently Mr. Ghosn listened to every presentation, how few words he spoke, and how calculated his questions were when he did speak. At the conclusion of the meeting, Mr. Ghosn addressed me politely and spoke to me briefly like a real person. I attempted to do the same in return with due respect. His entourage and his motorcade awaited, and he left. I did not know it at the time, but this conference, as well as my introduction to Mr. Ghosn, was a defining moment. It left a mark.

It is worth noting that Mr. Ghosn, who led not only Michelin but also Renault, AvtoVAS, Nissan, and Mitsubishi, has found himself in some hot water since 2018. I refuse to speculate on or contribute to the negative swirl around him, preferring rather to restate what I know to be positive. I don't know Mr. Ghosn beyond our singular group meeting and one personal introduction, each of which lasted no more than ninety and two minutes, respectively. I don't know if he is guilty of whatever has landed him in hot water or not. What I do know is that he was kind and courteous to me and appeared to be a man of intelligence and considerable business acumen. I'm thankful to have met him. We all make mistakes, and we all have reparations to make in some areas.

"That's all I have to say about that."
—Forrest Gump

"If you don't have anything nice to say,
don't say anything at all."
—Dad

In the twelve months or so that I spent in and out of the Michelin plant, I developed friendships with many good folks. Some of these friendships remain vibrant to this day. During this time at US2, I came to know that Michelin's only proving ground in North America is located about one hour from Clemson. By chance or divine providence, I also learned through one of Dad's insurance contacts that a young engineer named Brad was a test driver at the proving ground and that he would be happy to talk with me. None of this information, mind you, came by way of my own work or brilliance. It came just the same, and I was prepared to leverage the information and develop the contacts.

Fast-forward a few weeks and recall that I am a motorsports addict. Brad and I met as soon as I could find a spot in his schedule. We hit it off like two peas in a pod and could jabber endlessly about our shared interest. I suspected Brad would be a treasured asset and would develop into a good friend. He was and he did.

My project at Michelin was going well. I was deeply engaged, my work was bearing fruit, and most folks seemed to like me and my approach. I could see the light at the end of the tunnel of my graduate program, I had met Mr. Ghosn and his people, and I had begun a friendship with Brad at the proving ground. The stage, or perhaps the track, began to take shape in my mind's eye.

With perhaps three months remaining in my graduate program—thanks to my champion, Ken at GM—I was once again offered the opportunity to join General Motors upon graduation. I hadn't yet officially interviewed, but Ken assured me that the role would be a good one with the corporate environmental group. The position would be both lucrative and upwardly mobile. Starting salary was just under $50,000 in 1995, and it was within a rapidly expanding, high-profile group where $80,000 could be expected within eighteen months. Ken was aware that my research was with Michelin, but, up to this point, I don't believe he was aware that a proving-ground influence was creeping onto the scene.

Still a few months from project completion, Michelin, too, was kind enough to extend an interview opportunity in my direction. My research was ahead of schedule and under budget. It had borne real fruit, and I jelled with the workforce. Michelin was happy with me and with my project. In spite of my feelings of guilt for considering Michelin over GM after all GM had done for me, I was truly excited. I was eager for an opportunity to interview with Michelin. I wanted to work at the proving ground, and I wanted it badly. Such an opportunity to become a Michelin test driver was rare, and it would likely not return later if passed over at its first appearance. *Carpe diem* comes to mind. In rural Indiana vernacular,

Strike while the iron is hot.

To become a test driver on Michelin's team, one first had to be an engineer. The department was technically called *On-Vehicle Development Engineering*. As such, driving engineers needed to possess adequate skills behind the wheel, adhere to defined testing methods and processes, and communicate effectively with engineering counterparts at the various auto manufacturers. There were certainly conventional office interviews to assess communication skills, engineering aptitude, interpersonal skills, and the like, but none of these mattered if there was not sufficient instinct behind the wheel that could be developed.

My driving interview came first. I went into the interview with balanced and appropriate levels of both confidence and humility. I was drawing upon many years of experience behind the wheels, bars, and controls of everything from skid-steer loaders to boats. You'll recall that Dad had turned me loose on a barren, frozen lake at age twelve with a snowmobile capable of triple-digit speeds. Dad knew that we grow toward the high expectations we embrace for ourselves, and he allowed me to embrace high expectations early. I was comfortable with all past machinery and confident in my ability to quickly learn and adapt to anything new. I had no idea what to expect in the interview, and I remember very little of it beyond one misstep on my part. That one mistake made all other aspects of the day fade into the background.

At one point in the process, my would-be Michelin boss, also named Ken, directed me onto a track referred to as *B2* with a grumpy old blue 1989 Mustang GT five-speed wearing already-thrashed tires. B2 is a polished-concrete half-mile circle perhaps forty feet in width. It is bordered inside and outside by another ten or twelve feet of rough asphalt. Beyond the asphalt on both sides of the track was considerable additional width of stone. Within the first few feet of stone, both inside and outside the track, were concrete boxes. These concrete boxes concealed sprinkler heads that showered the track with water. The concrete boxes were supposed to be flush with the surface of the stone. Water from the sprinklers made the track slick, and the sporadic showers limited visibility. B2 was ornery, but it was a blast to attempt to master.

I was told to circle the track counterclockwise, working my way up to "the limit," which is the point of peak grip beyond which tires lose some amount of traction and the vehicle starts to slide. On this surface, with this vehicle setup, the limit was somewhere around 50 mph. Once I had demonstrated that I could safely find the limit and circle the track near that point, I was instructed to go beyond the limit and attempt to establish a steady drift, i.e., a tail-happy slide, around the track for as long as I could.

Things were going well. I was able to string together several significant segments of drift, improving smoothness and drift duration as I developed more and more comfort with the car. Going back to Dad's instruction, I started feeling that I "had it mastered." It certainly wasn't time to put it away, however, not here. In this role, I was expected to keep pushing, to keep improving. I did eventually spin out as every newbie does at some time on this track. Unfortunately, this particular spin was destined for trouble.

My slide trajectory took my right rear tire directly to one of those immovable concrete sprinkler boxes, one that happened to have a shortage of gravel in front of its leading edge. Ken and I in the old Mustang were almost stopped before we slid from the asphalt to the stone, but not quite. The right rear tire tagged the sprinkler box just hard enough, just high enough, to bend the aluminum wheel slightly and unseat the tire, resulting in a flat.

Ken acted as though it were no big deal. He praised the progress I had made and asked for my thoughts on what had transpired and why. I dissected the dynamics to the best of my ability as I hobbled the old horse back to the barn. I had certainly had a few miscues behind the wheel that contributed to the spin, but the spin trajectory toward a poorly backfilled sprinkler box just felt like bad luck. The incident did, however, deliver a dose of humility that did me some good. It wouldn't be my first or last dose of helpful humility, and it wasn't the death of my driving interview. Ken was cool about the whole thing and actually appeared fairly pleased with my performance. I think he was surprised I had ridden the old steed as long and as successfully as I had.

Next came the formal corporate interview at the "Crystal Palace," the headquarters building for Michelin North America in Greenville, South Carolina. I was proud of my research project, which was nearing its successful end, and I hoped that association with Mary Lou and meeting Mr. Ghosn would serve as feathers in my figurative cap. I was confident going into this interview. I wasn't looking to come off as cocky, but I knew what I wanted. I also knew I had a great opportunity with GM. With the exception of the bent wheel and flat tire, the driving portion of my interview had gone well days before, and I walked with confidence and moxie in my manner. I wore my only suit and finished it off with a Looney

Tunes Tasmanian Devil tie my sister had given me years before. I wasn't desperate, and I wasn't arrogant, but I was distinctly confident.

Why exactly I wore the Tasmanian Devil tie remains at least partially shrouded in mystery. I didn't have many ties, I was a Taz sort of guy, and I thought my sister might osmotically assist in some way and appreciate inclusion. I do recall at least one interviewer's being curious, taken aback, or perhaps shocked enough to ask about it. I remember responding with some answer involving confidence, being true to self, and being clear on what you want. These were statements with which Dad, Ken, Mary Lou, and others would all have agreed but perhaps delivered with a touch more reservation. Wearing the tie and responding without reservation or apology was probably a gamble. At Michelin, I wanted the job at the proving ground, only the job at the proving ground. It was the type of job where you seldom wore a tie, and, if you did, Taz would feel right at home.

The balance and the line I sought between confidence and bravado must have been understandable, or at least tolerable, to my interviewers. I was offered the job. It wasn't $50,000, but it was $45,000, almost $5000 more than they typically invested in new engineers fresh out of college at that time. Why did Michelin come forward with the extra $5000? It was because I believed what I had to offer was worth it, because I specifically asked for $5000 more, and because I explained that I was considering Michelin's path relative to another solid offer at almost $50,000 from GM. Even in our secular world, ask and you may receive. Fail to ask and you shall regret.

With confidence, ask for what you want.

With the coveted Michelin offer on the table, I had a new problem. It was a good problem, a problem where guidance from Dad would bring great relief. I had two outstanding job offers from two solid companies (offers no doubt extended to me in no small part with the help of people I admired). I wanted to express my appreciation by accepting each of their offers, but I could only choose one. As the old adage goes, "You can do anything you want in life, just not everything." On the one hand, General Motors and my friend and mentor, Ken, had been so good and generous to me for so long. They had invested many thousands of dollars and considerable time into me that could have instead been invested into other equally deserving engineers. On the other hand, my experience with Michelin up to that point had been very positive, and I was absolutely certain I would enjoy the too-good-to-be-true opportunity to become a test driver for the world's premier tire company.

I clearly recall sitting at my research desk at Michelin, feeling almost ill that I had to make a decision that would disappoint someone at this level. If I went with Michelin, I would be turning down the high-profile, steep-corporate-ladder job at GM and would be thumbing my nose at the company who had invested in me so generously. Maybe, I feared, I would erode trust and endanger my friendship with Ken. Perhaps our friendship and the opportunity to reconnect and "pay GM back" at some point in the future would be damaged or lost altogether. If I went with GM, I would be making good money with great opportunities for advancement. I would remain in a pool of scholarship recipients whose corporate-ascension ladders were often steeper than those of the populace. However, I feared that I would enjoy environmental-engineering work just as much in a corporate setting as I enjoyed it in an academic setting, meaning *not at all*. Finally, given the level of boldness I had displayed in charging after the test-driving job for Michelin, I felt certain the test-driving opportunity would never return once passed.

I knew at my core that I wanted to drive. I had been a motorsports fanatic for as long as I could remember. I didn't want to be a regular engineer, and I certainly didn't want to be an environmental engineer driving a desk and juggling regulations paperwork. It was difficult for me to actually say those words to my parents, to Ken, and to others who had poured into my academic education. I couldn't expect their full endorsement of the path so easily followed by the heart. My parents, GM, and I, too, had spent lots of money and almost 5½ college years pursuing normal, academic engineering. Normal engineering was supposed to bear my fruit. Test driving was not normal engineering, but it was real. I had met and conversed with those happy souls who did such work. Hope was born. Both my mind and my heart knew I could drive, and that's what I wanted to do.

As I sat at my desk, ineffectively attempting to find my way—or, more correctly, to find affirmation—I decided to "phone a friend," Dad.

He listened patiently from behind his own desk hundreds of miles away and returned words that brought instant relief and clarity. Dad is not a big talker, so his words were few in number, but his counsel overflowed with simple, priceless wisdom—to my racked spirit, pure gold. With his words, my narrow, slippery path instantly transformed into a vast, dry runway with tower reporting that I was clear for departure. "You'll always wonder from behind your corporate desk what might have been had you chosen the driving path. If you don't check that box now, you will probably regret it, and it will be difficult for you to ever fully commit yourself to anything else. You really have no choice." —Dad

Develop your gifts. Pursue what you love.
It will seldom seem like work.

Hanging up the phone, I reclined fully in my chair, almost to the point of falling over backward. I looked straight up at the ceiling and drew and released several deep breaths as the sheen on my eyes came up and dulled once again. I allowed a relieved smile to come over my countenance as I returned upright to face opportunities anew. A huge burden had been lifted with Dad's few words.

The next significant responsibility was to communicate my decision to Ken at GM. This communication needed to happen *before* accepting the offer from Michelin. This may seem backward in terms of risk or common practice, but in terms of respect, it was proper. I needed to talk with Ken before formally accepting the driving offer from Michelin. Doing so would give Ken the opportunity to explain alternatives or attempt to persuade me otherwise, before I was locked in to the Michelin path. Ken and GM absolutely deserved this opportunity to explain and persuade if they chose.

After explaining my situation, to my great relief, Ken was not openly disappointed, though he had every right to be. I'm sure the loyal GM man in him was disappointed, but he contained those feelings, instead allowing his car-guy core to relate and continue championing me, if not my decision. I thanked Ken profusely, did my best to maintain healthy relations with GM and preserve my valued friendship with Ken, and looked toward an exciting new chapter of life as a test driver. I accepted Michelin's offer.

The next few months were some of the longest, slowest-moving months of my life. I needed to finish my research project properly, write and defend my thesis, and throw off the academic shackles that confined me. I was to be a test driver. There were no work-arounds for my last tasks. No one else could do my academic push-ups. I had to man up and do the work, no matter how boring, no matter how much I hated chemistry, no matter how lame my findings seemed, no matter how much I felt like that square peg headed for life's ruthless reshaping lathe. Somehow, someway, I just had to get it done and get out.

Work first; play later.

By this point, my research project was well into its second phase of tackling one particular waste stream and attempting to recover valuable resources from that stream. I identified the exact piece of equipment I needed for collection and processing of waste-stream samples. Collecting and processing samples was, by far, the most important and time-consuming element of this second and final phase. The equipment package I needed looked like a miniature wastewater treatment plant, required maybe thirty to forty square feet of floor space, and was delivered by fork truck on several pallets. At the time, only one company in the country made anything like this, and it was not available for purchase, only for lease. It was exactly what I needed, but it would take some time to prepare, ship, set up, operate, and break down again for return.

Being well beyond eager, I innocently got myself into a slight pickle by going directly to the manufacturer without using the corporate purchasing process, where bids were requested of multiple suppliers, etc. Corporate purchasing requirements were new to me, and these administrative hassles could have meant lengthy delays if Mary Lou hadn't mercifully stepped in to help calm the waters. The item was ordered, and a painfully distant delivery date was set.

It seemed like an eternity, but I used the waiting time to prepare everything I could. I made sure that the unit arrived to a home already carved out in the basement bowels of one of the primary production buildings. Electrical, mechanical, and plumbing provisions were arranged and in order. I knew and optimized the process for analyzing samples by doing practice tests with untreated solutions of known concentration. I knew when I could access the lab and with whom I needed to work, no matter the hour. My trusty Chevy truck, outfitted with a tonneau cover, a sleeping mat, and a windup travel alarm clock, would serve as my on-site apartment for as much time as I could stand.

According to my sampling plan, I needed to pull and analyze samples at varying frequencies, depending upon concentrations of certain elements. Early in a process run, the samples were needed every two or three hours, but as the filtration system loaded up and approached its backwash cycle, I needed to pull samples more frequently, perhaps as frequently as every ten to fifteen minutes. The closer I could get to operation around the clock, the sooner I could finish collecting data. The sooner I could analyze and sort the data, the sooner I could complete and defend my thesis. The sooner I could defend my thesis, the sooner I could graduate and get to the track. Round-the-clock operation is exactly what I tried to pull off, for almost one month.

In the larger gaps early in a process run, I left for food, for exercise, for a shower, or perhaps for some sleep in the parking lot in the back of my truck. As the gaps got smaller near the end of a run, I sampled and analyzed, sampled and analyzed. I shut down as much as I could on Sundays for church, fellowship, and rejuvenation. Rain or shine, day or night, I sampled and analyzed. I'm sure I was a comical character. Like everyone else, I wore a dark blue standard-issue one-piece Michelin jumpsuit, only mine was different. Since I was only temporary, a student, my suits were loaners. They didn't have my name on them, but rather only an off-color, rectangular shadow where the previous owner's patch had been removed. In addition to my stylish garb, I was always snatching one of those fashionable three-wheeled factory bikes to haul sample bottles in the baskets, pedaling them up and down the hill to the lab, where I could analyze them. I must have looked something like Almira Gulch with Toto from *The Wizard of Oz*. I didn't care what people thought of how I dressed or how corny I looked. I have never cared about those things. I had to finish. I had to move on.

No matter what, finish!

CHAPTER 6

GRADUATION TO MICHELIN

Lessons on Friendship, Professor Bob, Used Nails,
and Investments behind the Scenes

WHILE I WAS CERTAINLY EAGER TO ASSUME MY TEST-DRIVER ROLE, I wasn't eager to move on from everything I had come to know and appreciate at Clemson and US2. Clemson is a great little college town in the foothills of the Smoky Mountains. It is a beautiful place with much to offer. The climate, the scenery, the roads, the multitudes of outdoor activities, and the pleasant people are all noteworthy. It really felt like home away from home.

Ron, Lamar, my good friends Rick and Mike, my grad school girlfriend Kim—each of these great people helped me in many ways and made the challenges of my project more bearable. As tough as that time was, and as much as I struggled to enjoy anything about my field of study, I certainly enjoyed these folks and appreciated their help and friendship. Filthy wastewater samples, paper routes, lawn mowing, gravy-slathered lunches, NASCAR races, trips to the lake, mountain biking, Clemson concerts, and challenges of manhood—there was always something of value to discuss, enjoy, or learn from this motley crew.

Then there was Bob. My dear friend Bob, Professor Bob, or "PB," as so many of his students referred to him, was one of the major reasons

Clemson is a special place for me. Behind my dad and my grandfather Clem (Dad's father), Bob poured more mentorship and love into my life than perhaps any other man. Bob has been my greatest motivation to finish this book promptly. Bob was ninety-one when I began my research and writing efforts. He was in reasonably good health and mentally sharp. That was more than five years ago. I haven't seen Bob in the years between. Our communications have been less frequent and more challenging because it became difficult for Bob to hear. It also seemed that he retracted a bit and sought visitation less and less as he got older. I wanted Bob to read these words, or perhaps have them read to him. I wanted Bob to understand his positive impact on me and to absorb my appreciation. My world is far richer because of him.

Statistically speaking, Bob wasn't supposed to make it. He was born very premature in 1924. At that time, most children so premature (born at twenty-eight weeks) would never have survived. He was barely thirty ounces at birth. *That's less than two pounds!* Bob's "diaper" in those earliest days was a cotton ball. His mother and aunt poured immeasurable love into his delicate being. They gave him every physical opportunity to survive. Survive, and thrive, he did. Bob grew to be not so delicate. At one time, he was well over six feet three inches tall, most of that in the legs. When Bob hugged folks, it was more like a bear hug. His beltline landed at chest level for most.

Standing tall in the midst of the Greatest Generation, Bob was a proud sailor, having served his country honorably during a dangerous era, including service in WWII. He would tell me stories now and again of his Navy days, his duties on the ship, and how he got to be so proficient at ironing clothing crisply. He told me about divine intervention into one of his ship assignments at the eleventh hour, an assignment that removed him from the ship shortly before it set sail. Tragically, it would be that ship's final voyage. Within days, the ship sank, taking every sailor down with it. Had Bob been on that ship, you would not be reading these words.

When I got to Clemson in the fall of 1993, one of my first orders of business was to connect with the Catholic community on campus, to begin attending masses, and to serve in some productive way. At the time, Bob was a mentor and trainer to church members who wanted to serve the parish as readers, or lectors. Being a college professor, Bob was an excellent reader and speaker, so it was only natural that he would mentor new folks, particularly incoming students, on the finer points. Bob was also the most senior professor I have ever heard of. An engineering graduate of Carnegie Mellon many moons ago, Bob started teaching engineering classes at Clemson after returning from the Navy in September 1947. In 1993, when I matriculated, he was starting his forty-seventh year. Bob continued teaching until 2009, an amazing legacy of instruction spanning sixty-two years at one university.

I met Bob for the first time in the lobby of Saint Andrew Catholic Church. We arranged to go through the lector procedures and iron out a few administrative details. With no foreknowledge or purpose, I wore one of my Pi Kappa Alpha fraternity shirts to the meeting on that particular evening. Bob noticed. With a distinct sparkle in his eye and a resolute grip of his hand, he pulled me into the handshake and greeting known only to brothers. I was taken aback. Here was this tall, imposing, older man grabbing my hand with resolve and welcoming me as a brother. That was the start of a long and treasured friendship.

Bob reminded me of the importance of pauses and tone changes in my reading and of maintaining eye contact with the congregation. He celebrated my successes and moved quickly beyond my failures. He told little jokes, made little jabs, and unleashed his strange, endearing comedy with regularity, whether I got his humor or not. Bob shook hands and hugged as if it might be his last exchange. Bob and I grew quite close. His door and his heart were always open. We shared Papa John's pizza many Sunday evenings after church, along with details of our families, our lives, and our experiences. Bob listened much more than he spoke.

I had no reason to seek an additional father figure in my life. My biological father was larger than life and always available to me, though, at that time, physically distant by many miles. It wasn't until I came to know Bob that I was really able to appreciate additional sources of male leadership, wisdom, and mentorship in my life. I was away from home—really away from home—and Bob was always there. Bob's contribution and role in my life grew and changed, but it never diminished. While Bob was important to me during my time at Clemson, he became even more important in the chapters that followed.

Bob regularly reminded me to be thankful for my blessings, to be accepting of my station, and to always do my best, no matter the task or the calling. His mantra sounded a lot like guidance from Luke's twelfth chapter referenced earlier: "Much will be required of the person entrusted with much, and still more will be demanded of the person entrusted with more" (Luke 12:48). In that particularly difficult season of life at Clemson, such words both convicted and encouraged me. I had been granted both the ability and the opportunity to pursue an advanced degree. Though my chosen field had proven not to be the best fit for me, I had the responsibility to see my degree through to completion.

> "With ability comes responsibility."
> —Bob

As the time for my thesis defense approached, on a quiet Saturday morning, Bob took me to a quaint little men's store in downtown Clemson. The staff was enlivened with his appearance. Each called him by name. Bob oversaw as the manager selected and fitted a finely crafted white shirt to my frame and liking. Bob never looked or inquired about the price; he simply provided a proper garment he felt I needed. Once ready, he personally pressed it to his standard of naval perfection. Such was Bob's way.

On a sunny, picturesque afternoon in the spring of 1995, wearing my fine, crisply pressed shirt and a snuggly drawn tie, I presented and defended my thesis. Mary Lou was there, Dr. White was there, and Dr. Farley was there. They listened not in appreciation of academic genius or originality. Of that there was little. They listened not to seize upon any academic weakness they could exploit. There were many. Rather, they listened in appreciation of the effort, of the practical project findings that could be acted upon to reduce cost and minimize waste, and of the positive relationships developed. They asked several manageable questions and commented on a few of my methods. In the end, they accepted my thesis and its defense. They opened the door of my holding cell. I would soon graduate with my master's degree and move on.

I remember the relief I felt as I emerged from that building and loosened my tie to the afternoon sun on my face and neck. I did not throw in the towel, ring the bell, or tap out. I refused to quit. I finished well, and

I was free. The name *Geswein* was on an actual book, and not as a gimme or a gift. I earned it.

Dad had repeated the second grade probably because he was distracted by farmwork at home or by pestering little girls at school. He had never gone to college, but he could savor this moment with me because he knew what I had invested. He knew what I had sacrificed to achieve it. Had this been Dad's project, he would have slept in his truck, too. That's why they were there, waiting at my apartment. Mom and Dad were there to congratulate and celebrate with me. We were all ready for life's exciting new chapter to begin.

My first day at Michelin was May 30, 1995, a Tuesday. I remember the peace I felt. I belonged there, finally. The day went well. It was both surreal and natural at the same time. It was a bit hard to believe, in fact, that this was actually considered a job and that I was paid well to do it. I called home. I called Bob. A great new chapter was beginning.

In the weeks before starting work, I had found a small place just outside Laurens, South Carolina. It was a simple, small A-frame back in the woods about seven minutes from town and fifteen minutes from work. Another young engineer named Gene, who was with Milliken & Company, was already there on the lower level, but the upper level was available. Shared rent was $175 each. My books and files were in plastic milk crates. With a board stretched across my crates, I could sit cross-legged on the floor under the board to work at my makeshift desk.

Within a few months, Gene pursued other opportunities. He and his dog moved out, and I had the place all to myself. My landlord, Marshall, and his wife, Gerri, lived in one of the two houses out front, just up the lane from mine. His daughter, Leanne, and her husband, Doug, lived in the other. They are all great people with whom I became close friends, perhaps more like family, over the years. I had a job I loved, two well-earned engineering degrees under my belt, and a simple little place in the woods surrounded by good folks. I was making decent money, and I had hope. Life was pretty good at twenty-four.

Now that they were empty nesters with plenty of disposable income, Mom and Dad traveled more. I enjoyed having them visit and engage in my world in South Carolina. We took trips into the mountains. We joined Bob for church, and they met many of my new friends. I was able to get them into the proving ground after hours to show them around and take them on a few thrill rides. In spite of Mom's constant worry about the risks she perceived in my job, I knew my parents were happy.

I've already suggested that Dad is frugal and financially conservative. Both adjectives could easily be exchanged for stronger synonyms. I make these statements with a sense of pride. Dad will process them in the same sense without embarrassment or apology. Dad's defensive approach is one of the reasons he is where he is today with the flexibility to do the things he does. He lives in a comfortable facility with few financial concerns and is generous at every turn.

As a kid, I clearly recall helping Dad denail used lumber. The scene usually included two sawhorses and a considerable stack of lumber recovered from one of his recent demo projects or, more often, collected from the project of an acquaintance who failed to see the value in used building materials. There would be two buckets under or near the sawhorses. One was to collect junk that couldn't be recovered; the other was for the "good" nails that Dad was able to extract and straighten. Finally, there would be a pile of clean lumber growing like a well-earned callus with each stick Dad completed and tossed that direction.

Dad certainly could have bought fresh lumber and new nails; it wasn't about that. Why go to all this time and effort only to net secondhand material? Dad had time available. It was good exercise. He was capable, and he enjoyed the accomplishment. He didn't care what others thought of this simple work, and he ended up with adequate, free materials and a sense of satisfaction in knowing that he was alive and well.

It was in this very spirit that I approached my landlord, Marshall—a calm, kindly Southern gentleman—with a simple request in that exciting summer of 1995. I suggested that perhaps I should disassemble an old homemade 22' × 30' cedar carport from the back corner of my rental property in order to reconstruct it just off the back porch of the A-frame. In this way, I could provide shelter to my truck and other toys. Besides, the value of his rental property would only increase as a result of the relocation and refresh. A tiny outbuilding with electricity, snakes, and furry critters was located adjacent to the original location of the carport, so, in the same conversation, I also asked if I could commandeer and reconfigure this little gem as my workshop.

Usage of the little shanty as my workshop was a no-brainer to which

Marshall quickly gave approval. To the question of disassembling the dilapidated carport, uprooting its poles, ripping it free from its kudzu moorings and ivy vines, and reconstructing it near my A-frame, Marshall looked at me silently at some length as if to question whether or not I was actually serious, then shifted his gaze to the ground in contemplation. His slightly raised brow and gently shaking head foreshadowed the passive acceptance I was expecting. He raised his head. Words followed: "If you want to, but I sure wouldn't do it."

Those words sounded a lot like "Yes" to me. They were all I needed. Paul Geswein's second son had a construction project. Within two weeks, I had a functional carport for a grand total of $0.73. Actually, it was $1.00 since I tipped the guy at the hardware store the $0.27 balance for keeping his doors open a few extra minutes for me. Had I been a little more careful pulling and straightening nails, I might have gotten by with $0.00.

Some months later, the shade of this refreshed carport provided the cool, comfortable backdrop for another life lesson of great value. I was already well versed in our family's approach to spending, but on this particular occasion, I learned more of my parents' wisdom as it related to investing and generosity. Mom and Dad were down for a short visit. We were sitting in and around a hammock stretched between two posts of the carport. They focused my attention and began to explain that a season of life had been reached where my siblings and I could be expected to properly manage money from some investment accounts they had created years before, when we were kids. My siblings and I had been aware neither of these accounts nor of the fact that Mom and Dad had been sacrificing along the way to contribute to them. The accounts had grown large and useful. Mom and Dad's introduction of these accounts was an unexpected, pleasant surprise. The accounts were explained and presented in a way that ruled out any debate on the matter. Appreciative acceptance was the only option. There was no room for polite refusal of this gesture and no reason to do so. This was an occasion to simply say thank you and count our blessings for intelligent, thoughtful, frugal parents.

Work hard. Invest wisely. Invest early.
Count blessings more than dollars.

The money went to help fund new homes being built by my siblings for their growing families. I reinvested the dollars from my account into slightly more aggressive funds since I didn't imagine needing the money immediately. Reflecting on this story serves as a good reminder. Although we seldom realize or acknowledge it when we are young, we only know so much, sometimes pitifully little. None of us is self-made. There are folks helping us, praying for us, acting for us, investing in and for us. They are often behind the scenes, seeking no reward but the satisfaction of bringing joy.

Perhaps my story seems idyllic and unrepresentative. I understand that. Perhaps it is. Recall that I started my book by stating that I am a man of rich blessings and good fortune. I know I have been richly blessed. If your situation is much harder and devoid of love and support from the people around you, perhaps even from your earthly father, hang in there. You cannot change your past, but you absolutely can affect your future in a positive way. Wherever you are, whatever or whomever you have or don't have, it's all part of your life experience and can be leveraged for good. Cling to your heavenly Father, Who always seeks the best for you.

"For I know well the plans I have in mind for you, says the Lord, plans for your welfare, not for woe! plans to give you a future full of hope." (Jeremiah 29:11)

CHAPTER 7

SPEEDING THROUGH DIPS AND THORNS

Lessons on Red Corvettes, Replacing Socks, Love,
Loss, and Venom-Filled Sugar Cookies

As MY DRIVER TRAINING PROGRESSED, I BECAME CONVINCED THAT I HAD more than just passion for driving; I also had genuine aptitude. I'm certain that some measure of whatever skill I have can be traced back to Dad's starting us early and Mom's tolerance. We grew up riding and driving anything and everything we could get our hands on. Each machine, each experience, taught us something, something that sticks like the confidence and muscle memory that come from learning to ride a bike.

In the mid-1990s, a few times a year, Michelin's team of subjective test drivers ventured beyond our own proving grounds for high-speed testing and driver training at tracks such as Road Atlanta, Roebling Road, Nelson Ledges, Carolina Motorsports Park, and Virginia International Raceway. Ascent in this role at that time was no gimme. Drivers had to be fast, consistent, and safe. Drivers had to earn their place. Newbies had to start on the bottom rung of the ladder. I was good with that. I wouldn't have wanted it any other way.

With the help of Brad, my first friend at the track, and Dan, the group's patriarch and one of its faster drivers, I had been preparing for months on our home track. I had honed my skills in smaller, slower vehicles. I had demonstrated proficiency, safety, and judgment in midlevel performance cars (including that grumpy old '89 Mustang) and was pushing my training forward in the faster cars. I believed I was ready to put my skills to the test at one of the world's premier road courses: Road Atlanta, near Braselton, Georgia.

This first trip to Road Atlanta may end up going down as the most memorable experience of my driving career. Road Atlanta is a beautiful, fast, winding track with lots of elevation change and notable risk. The course flows naturally and is easy to learn, even though at least two of its corners are blind. What Road Atlanta is not is a track for the faint of heart, at least not back in the midnineties, before the Dip—its greatest and most memorable feature—was removed in the name of safety. Sometimes referred to as *Gravity Cavity*, the Dip and the track features that immediately followed it were absolutely exhilarating and had a way of separating the best from the rest.

In your mind's eye, imagine the slow, clunky, mechanical climb and the click, click, click of the linkages and safety catches bringing you and your train of cars to the apex of the biggest hill on a large roller coaster. From this peak, the mechanical sounds cease, replaced by the sounds of rushing wind and human emotion. You and your screaming cohorts are set free, stomachs seeming to rise and turn as you plunge ever faster and more steeply down toward the bottom of a massive drop. Soon you will be compressed hard into your seat as the speeding collection of cars reaches the bottom and is snatched immediately back up the face of the next hill. The Dip at Road Atlanta was an experience not so different from that coaster plunge from the highest point, down to the lowest point, then right back up the face of another hill. Road Atlanta's Dip wasn't as steep as that of a coaster, though perhaps it dropped as far. There were other factors, however, that made it far more exciting.

First, there was no slow, clunky coaster approach. Instead, drivers arrived at the Dip already "hauling the mail." The Dip was positioned at the end of a long, mostly straight backstretch. There was lots of space to build lots of speed headed for the Dip. Upon arrival at the Dip, drivers plunged downward as fast as possible without the position certainty afforded by a set of coaster rails. For most passenger cars at that time, the entry speed was somewhere around 130 mph before dropping into the Dip. If this feature still existed, performance cars today would likely reach at least 180 mph upon entry. A number of thoroughbred race cars would be well into the 200s. (The Dip was removed in 1997 to prevent faster cars from taking flight!)

Second, the Dip wasn't straight. Instead, the track transitioned distinctly left just after its lowest point while vehicles climbed the next hill. The descent into the Dip was exhilarating, to be sure, but driver separation happened while climbing hard and braking *very* late on the face of the far-side hill before a blind crest. This whole section of track was fast and dicey. Its finale was blind and bordered by immovable concrete walls. It was the most fun I had ever had behind the wheel of anything up to that point in my life.

I learned the features and details of this wonderful track quickly. I was earning my way up through the feeder cars into the faster stuff. By the third day of this first trip, I had earned my way to the big iron. On the afternoon of this third day, the door was finally opened for me to step into the fastest car in attendance that day, a 1993 Corvette on oversized BFGoodrich R1 race tires. I was in sync with that car and posted the fastest laps of the day for the whole group—much to their surprise. I was consistently finding areas to shave more time, going faster and faster with each successive lap. Everyone was on the pit wall watching, stopwatches in hand, waiting for the Vette to appear out of the final turn and race to the stripe in search of another tenth of a second or two. How much faster would each lap get? Everyone was on notice, particularly the senior drivers.

We closed out that afternoon a few laps early. The Georgia heat, the oversized race tires, the relentless lapping, and my aggression had sent coolant temperature to an unsafe level, and it was time to give the trusty Vette a break. Good thing, I suppose, because I was starting to think I had it mastered. When I called home from the hotel that evening, I couldn't have been on a higher cloud. This was happening. This was real. I had an actual gift for performance driving. It was an awesome natural high! I don't recall being able to share my joy directly with Dad because Mom answered. She was happy for me, certainly, but more thankful that nothing had gone wrong. If FaceTime had existed back then, I would have heard her words of congratulation, but I would have seen the distress on her person.

The mid to late 1990s were wonderful years in many ways. Mom and Dad were healthy, mostly retired, traveling more, and enjoying the fruits of their labors. They were enjoying each other, their grandkids from my siblings, and the high points in the lives of those they loved. It was the start of a sadly small but precious collection of golden years.

My job was exciting and challenging every day. It included just enough travel and flextime to spend at least a full week at home during every major holiday. For almost one month every winter, we performed our testing for snow performance in the Upper Peninsula of Michigan. Dad, my brother, and his boys would all come stay in my hotel room for several days, going snowmobiling by day and enjoying family time by night.

Back in South Carolina, I regularly traveled from Laurens to Clemson to enjoy church, pizza, and fellowship with Bob. It was not uncommon in those years to drive test cars home in the evening, and occasionally on weekends, to stay sharp on each car's idiosyncrasies and to give it some love. In addition to the enjoyment and fine tuning this provided and the TLC the cars often received, driving them home also meant that, occasionally, I could take Bob to church in something he would otherwise never experience. Sometimes they were ordinary minivans. Sometimes they were rugged trucks. Sometimes they were luxurious sedans. In those times when they were sporty, our church travels had some spice. The return usually concluded with a spirited lap around Bob's block, much to the displeasure of his neighbors, I'm sure.

BOB AND THE PORSCHE 944 IN HIGHLANDS, NC, CIRCA 1997

One particular weekend adventure is etched in my memory as I'm sure it is in Bob's. I had a Porsche 944 S2 home for some overdue TLC. The Sunday of that weekend was beautiful, and my detailing work was complete. I called Bob to see if he was available for a few extra hours before church. I failed to elaborate on the details of my plan, suspecting he might decline if he were fully in the know.

I picked him up at his home in Clemson, shoehorned him into the passenger side, and headed into the mountains toward Highlands, North Carolina. This is one of the more beautiful and exciting sections of road in our great land. Twists and turns for much of the hour-long trip tested Bob's bladder and stomach. He didn't say much. He also didn't relinquish his grip on the door handle and console until we reached Highlands. He may not have enjoyed the trip, but he endured, and he didn't complain. He made it. I would like to think that Bob developed a deeper appreciation of my love for driving and perhaps a better understanding of my job that day. To be honest, however, I think perhaps he just endured. He experienced life, shared his time, and participated in strengthening bonds and forming memories. You were a trouper, Bob. I always enjoyed keeping you on the edge of your seat.

Some months later, I paid Bob an unexpected visit at his home on a Saturday morning about an hour before an autocross was to be held in a parking lot at the base of Memorial Stadium. I, along with a few other Michelin drivers, represented Michelin in the autocross. I drove a newer, modified Mustang GT from the track, which desperately needed a bath and some TLC. It was important to me that Michelin show well both in terms of my performance and in terms of the Mustang's cosmetics. I certainly wanted to visit Bob, but my ulterior motive was to borrow water and some washing supplies to shine the galloping steed prior to the event. He didn't say so, but Bob's actions clearly articulated this instruction:

Good call. Details and professionalism are important. Always look and do your best.

There in his driveway, in stocking feet, at seventy-something years old, Bob helped me wash and dry that Mustang. He bid me good luck and farewell with his familiar friendly wave and salutation as I drove off just in the nick of time to make registration. With a smile and some measure of appreciative guilt, I left him there in his driveway to clean up, put away supplies, and change into dry socks. The Mustang and I went on to set the fastest time of the day, looking good in the process. Like so many great lessons he taught by example, Bob's lesson from that morning stuck with me:

Never pass up an opportunity to serve and teach in the moment. You can always buy more socks.

Around this time, two new drivers joined the team at Michelin: Kip and Brian. Kip turned out to be a fraternity brother of mine who had graduated from Clemson, though I didn't know or encounter him there. Kip actually had Bob as a professor in one of his engineering courses some years earlier and spoke very highly of our mutual friend—small world. Kip is a spirited, eclectic engineer. He is an academic driver, a wonderful human being, and a great friend. He is not a ragged-edge competitor behind the wheel. Brian, on the other hand, is that ragged-edge driver, with whom I developed a particularly strong friendship and quest for competition. Brian is an excellent driver, someone I needed for healthy challenge as I started getting comfortable at the top. We competed, raced, competed, razzed each other, and competed some more. It really didn't matter what the competition was. Driving, running, lifting weights, or shooting baskets, Brian and I were both ready and willing to engage in solid competition for the improvement of both. Kip, Brian, and Brian's parents became part my treasured collection of family and friends almost immediately. These are folks who would stick by me, trusted friends on whom I could count, no matter what. Such times of requisite support would arrive all too soon.

THREE AMIGOS: BRIAN AND I WITH HIS DAD, LARRY, CIRCA 1998

As our friendship developed, Brian, his dad Larry, and I began racing together. First, it was autocross and instruction at driving schools throughout the southeast. Soon we added road racing in the Sports Car Club of America (SCCA), and, shortly thereafter, we stepped up to the

Grand American Cup Series, and One Lap of America. Brian's Dodge Neon ACR might spend one weekend on a track such as Road Atlanta or VIR, outfitted with a full cage and one suspension setup, only to have us remove the cage and reset the suspension and alignment settings after work during the week to be ready for an autocross somewhere the next weekend. That back-and-forth process repeated itself more times than either of us can recall. We slept in Larry's race trailer, in tents, in my support car, and in an actual hotel on rare occasions. Larry snored like a freight train, no matter the venue.

Brian's beloved dog, Chelsea, was a faithful teammate, as well. She passed gas regularly. On one occasion, she sheepishly lowered her guilt-ridden, powder-covered face when we returned from a morning driver's meeting. She had eaten our morning doughnuts. On most weekends, our routine included pizza one night and Cracker Barrel the other. We also supplemented an abundance of candy orange slices, no matter the hour, to ensure we were properly sugared up. We had a blast and became the closest of friends.

By the early 2000s, Brian and I had become at least somewhat recognizable in name, in face, or perhaps in both in some motorsports circles. On occasion, we were called upon individually to represent two of the biggest and best names in aftermarket performance. I met and had the opportunity to drive for John Lingenfelter and the Lingenfelter Performance Engineering team, while Brian drove for John Hennessey and his group at Hennessey Performance. Behind the wheel, we were entrusted with the reputations of these great tuners and thousands of horsepower worth hundreds of thousands of dollars. It was a great honor for each of us.

Before racing headlong and waist-deep into additional driving reflections, it is important to introduce a very special woman to this testosterone-heavy chronicle. In the summer of 1998, at the age of twenty-seven, in the midst of all this career and racing excitement, I finally met the one and only woman for me. Our meeting was blind for me and mostly blind for her. Several friends and family members had attempted to set me up in the past—many times, in fact. Previously, none had come even remotely close to success. My brother, Shawn, however, who had never once set me up before, suggested that I meet Tekoa as part of a double date on the lake. Shawn was a ladies' man all through high school and into his Air Force career, so with nothing more than his assuring words, "Trust me," I agreed.

From that very first day on the lake, I knew there was something special about Tekoa, something for which I had been searching and was ready. Only a few days later, following my first genuine solo date with Tekoa, Mom predictably unfurled the "So, how did it go?" question scroll. Her jaw hit the proverbial floor when I clearly stated that Tekoa was the woman I intended to marry. Nothing, nothing, nothing for years, then one real date at age twenty-seven, and that was it, at least for me.

Tekoa and I enjoyed a few more evenings together that week in the summer of 1998, but by Friday, something had changed for her. She was not in the same place I was, and she didn't want to deepen the relationship any further with the prospect of my return to South Carolina in only a few days. Tekoa was just twenty-two, South Carolina was too far away, and she wasn't comfortable developing a deep relationship so fast. She shared her concerns and told me she thought it would be better to just be friends. Instead of moving forward with the plans we had made for another date that Friday evening, with a shocked and heavy heart, I watched her drive away.

I was deflated. The time I had hoped to spend with Tekoa, introducing her to my family and sharing our Fourth of July traditions the next day, was instead spent gazing blankly into the night sky. Firework twinkles and distant reports were barely perceptible from the bottom of the pit I was in. My body was there, and my eyes were looking up, but I was somewhere else. My parents saw the peak of happiness and the valley of sadness I experienced in the span of one week. I didn't want more friendly friends, and I told her so. I had enough of those. I wanted my forever best friend. In time, I wanted her as my wife, though I certainly didn't share that depth with her then. I knew I could love this woman, but she couldn't love me back.

I don't recall anything Dad might have said in those dark days. It's a shame because I'm sure whatever he might have said was of considerable value. I was tuned out, but I know Dad was tuned in. Many years before, in his courting days, Dad had had to win over my mom. It had not been a simple matter for him. He had worked for her and had reached a point where Mom was either going to go out with him and give him a shot, or he was moving on. Dad knew that Tekoa's departure was a huge loss for me, but there was nothing either of us could do.

I still had everything I had before meeting Tekoa. I had a wonderful life, but I didn't have her. On that Friday night, shortly before she drove off with the suggestion that we be friends, I affectionately, but resolutely, told her that she would not hear from me. I didn't want or need more regular friends. I told her how strongly I felt for her and that, should her situation change and should she want to reach out to me, I would be happy to hear from her. She would not hear from me until then. I returned to South Carolina saddened, but not without hope. I reengaged the great life I had going previously, but with a Tekoa-shaped gap. Once the mind and heart are expanded to appreciate something new and treasured, they will not return unaffected to their former conditions. I was forever changed.

Bob was back in South Carolina, ever ready to listen, ever ready to support. I was tuned out to his wisdom, as well. I don't recall his words; I just remember him listening to my words, sharing friendship, fellowship, pizza, and spice drops. Closing each visit, Bob would send me off Laurens-bound with his signature bear hug, his endearing Forrest Gump wave, and his familiar closing words of support: "Love and prayers, my boy, love and prayers. Bye-bye."

Brian and Larry certainly knew the highlights of my ups and downs with Tekoa, but I didn't elaborate, and we didn't dwell. We moved quickly past, we continued to compete, we continued to race, we continued to enjoy this special season of life and bond through shared experiences. Bob would listen and smile as I regaled him with our tales of racing and adventure. We raced Brian's Neon in Kansas at the ProSolo nationals and our Golf GTI at tracks throughout the southeast. At one point, we smoked the engine in the GTI, and Bob kindly kicked in $1000 to help with replacement costs.

I would be remiss not to continue painting the picture of Bob's generous legacy, though perhaps a bit out of order chronologically. In the early spring of 2000, when I foolishly decided to purchase my first brand-new anything (a 2000 Honda 929RR crotch rocket), Bob pulled another $1000 from his wallet to ensure that I was riding well equipped: full leathers, gloves, helmet—the whole shooting match. His generosity continues to this day. Shouldn't we all have such supportive and generous friends? Shouldn't we all *be* such supportive and generous friends?

Back into the late nineties, I bought another Corvette, this time a red 1993 coupe with a six-speed. It wasn't brand new, of course, but I paid cash, and it was all mine. I remember driving this one home from South Carolina for a holiday. I hadn't told Mom and Dad about this car. I just showed up with it.

My first Corvette, the 1968 still sitting in Dad's garage, was only driven occasionally on nice, sunny summer days; it was a garage queen. The '93, on the other hand, was to be enjoyed, more like how Dad had enjoyed the Vettes of his youth. It wasn't long before Dad and I enjoyed my '93 together on a trip to one of the biggest annual Corvette events in the world: Bloomington Gold. We had a blast. As much fun as I was having, and as much success as I was enjoying otherwise in life, still, there was the Tekoa gap. No amount of money, no amount of success, neither experience, nor drug, nor drink, nor elixir of any kind can change this fact:

The best things in life aren't things.

Driving was going well, really well—perhaps too well. As Dad and my grandpa both might say, I was unwittingly "getting too big for my breeches." "Son, once you think you've got it mastered, you better put it away," Dad regularly reminded. At the root of all but one crash for which I've ever been responsible in my life is my failure to heed this bit of Dad's wisdom. The time for correction was at hand. God felt it necessary to adjust the attitude of this spirited son in the form of a Viper crash.

The venerable Dodge Viper became publicly available in 1991. Michelin did not have a Viper in its fleet at Laurens until the late nineties. I was a Corvette man, for sure, but I was also a huge fan of the Viper from my very first exposure. I loved its raw, audacious, in-your-face style, its massive V10 engine, its standard six-speed manual transmission, its absence of driving aids, and its excuses for nothing. If you didn't like the Viper, that was fine. You could jolly well find yourself a lesser car. This was the essence and appeal of the Viper, raw and unapologetic.

First-generation Vipers, and most of the second generation, had no anti-lock braking system (ABS), no traction control, and no stability control. There were no training wheels, no "helpers in the car" to drive for you if you got in over your head. Since the side exhaust ran directly beneath the door sills, if you weren't careful, you could burn yourself getting in and out of the beast. Early Vipers were the pit bulls of the automotive landscape, bulging, visceral, masculine, powerhouses of the era. They required strong, confident controllers to extract their greatness. Many of the cars also had a ghostly issue with the brakes. In certain conditions, with little warning, the brakes of affected Vipers would simply take a break—pardon the pun. For a brief moment, the surprised operator was left with limited options: identify the least damaging path, commit that direction, and pray—quickly!

MY FIRST EXPOSURE TO THE VIPER—I'M HOOKED, CIRCA 1998

Our senior driver, Dan, had been in charge of the Chrysler OE account for years. This meant that all original-equipment North American tire programs that involved testing for Chrysler brand, which included Dodge and Jeep, channeled through Dan. Dan was well respected by folks at Chrysler and had logged many laps at speed in a Viper. He knew the car's character well. He was also changing roles and transferring Chrysler-account responsibility over to Brian. Dan was instrumental in my training. Both Dan and Brian knew I possessed the skills needed to drive the Viper. When a Viper on long-term loan from Dodge finally arrived at the track,

Dan and Brian allowed me to drive it in spite of the fact that I wasn't connected directly with Chrysler or Dodge in the way that they were.

On one fateful afternoon several weeks after we took delivery of the Viper, I was out turning some spirited laps on various circuits, as was my routine. It was later in the day, after many had already left for home. Staying late to practice in something different was my routine almost daily. It was Brian's routine, as well. We often practiced together. This particular day, I had gotten their permission to practice with the Viper, but neither Brian nor Dan was physically with me. I was exploring a bit more with each lap, feeling in complete harmony with this wonderful car. I say "spirited" laps because they were not full-out max-handling laps. If they were, I would have pulled out all but the last few stops. I would have been required to wear a helmet and driving suit, use the full racing harness, and have a medical standby. These were instead honest-to-goodness spirited laps. To the untrained, such laps would have seemed like max-handling laps, but they were not. They were more like 85%–90% laps. There was plenty of remaining margin for error or malfunction.

Few others beyond Dan and Brian had any sort of exposure to the car, let alone exposure north of 80%, where the car's true brilliance shone forth. In my joy and confidence, I wanted to share the experience before concluding for the day, so my friend John jumped in with me for a few more laps. Connect my excitement with my bravado, then add an excitable passenger. With this concoction, perhaps I began moving toward that 90%–95% zone. John, an avid and skilled motorcycle rider, was literally hooting, hollering, and gyrating in the right seat as we lapped the track. He was amazed at the car's aptitude and my willingness to demonstrate with laps at this pace. His enthusiasm and appreciation just fanned the flames of my ego. My self-talk probably ran along the lines of "I've got this." In expanded form, "I've got this mastered." Figurative storms brewed.

Shortly after dropping John off from his handful of laps, I accosted my brother Kip, who was staying a few minutes later than normal: "Kip, you've got to come check this out." Jumping into a Viper by my urging to "come check this out" was not Kip's nature. Remember, Kip is the academic, the not-so-ragged-edge driver. Kip trusted me, his adrenaline-rich, Taz-tie-sporting, bungee-jumping friend and fraternity brother. We were barely a lap into our experience at the same spirited pace I was enjoying just a few minutes earlier with John when we came to the braking zone for the "parking lot turn" on Track 2. On approach to this corner, we needed to brake from perhaps 105 mph down to 55 or 60 to be able to make the corner. I went for the brakes, or so I thought. We were not slowing down, and the corner was approaching—rapidly.

Did I miss something? Had I just driven too deeply into the braking zone in all of my excitement? No time for analysis. Doesn't matter now. Hang on, Kip. We are going off straight.

Rather than trying to make the corner, I decided to go off straight and minimize damage to the car, including the possibility of a larger crash or rollover. We bumped and bounced along the gravel and the grass that surrounded the track, trying to scrub as much speed as possible and keep the car going straight toward the lowest, least damaging obstruction in our path: a bramble-filled swale between two large earthen embankments. We were still doing probably 35 or 40 mph when we reached the brambles. We stopped, sure enough, with dirt, dust, dry bramble leaves, and berries still settling onto and inside the car. No one was hurt. We were straight, we were upright, and there was no major impact, just a bumpy ride into a very inhospitable "catch fence."

I shut the car off, looked at Kip in dumbfounded amazement, and prepared to climb out the window Hazzard-style. I became acutely aware of the ticking sounds from hot components not given the courtesy of a cooldown lap. I was also acutely aware of the smell of hot, dry foliage beneath the car and acutely aware of the layer of dirt, dust, and berries covering the whole car and, to some degree, the interior and its occupants. I was acutely aware of the bramble thorns, the scratches, and the disappointment in myself for my lapse in judgment and for whatever procedural mistake I had made behind the wheel.

With a radio call to the security team, in short order, we extracted the car straight back out from where I had augered it into the brambles. I drove it back to the shop, swept it out, and cleaned it up the best that I could. I made some phone calls. I don't recall the exact timing, but I do recall following Dan's guidance to drive the car yet that evening to Greenville. I dropped it off where the Michelin mechanics at the research shop could look it over and repair whatever needed to be repaired in the coming days.

The joy I had felt during my first-ever Viper drive was conspicuous by its absence on this drive to the big shop in Greenville. I wanted a full reboot. I wanted everything to just be okay. I wanted the slate wiped back clean as if nothing had ever happened. I should have listened better. "Son, once you think you've got it mastered, you better put it away." I did think I had it mastered, and I should have put it away.

My mistakes that afternoon drained a measure of trust from the personal accounts I had built with some folks very important to me, Dan and Brian topping that list. It also put Michelin, Dan, and Brian in particular, in the unfair and uncomfortable predicament of having to explain to Dodge why this Viper, on loan to Michelin, even after cleanup, checkout, and realignment, might no longer be suitable for testing. How could anyone know it hadn't been compromised in some undetectable way that might negatively affect test results or endanger someone's safety? I felt sick and responsible. I was responsible.

To this day, I still cannot say exactly what happened. I can say there was only one guy behind the wheel: me.

Kip and I went out in a Porsche early the next morning, before work. At the same speed, on the same track, I started braking from the same point where witness marks could be seen from the previous afternoon. From that point, in the Porsche, we were able to stop completely before the corner, let alone being able to slow only to 55 or 60 mph. That wasn't proof of innocence, however. All this really indicated was that I had started braking plenty early on most of my laps half a day before. It didn't guarantee that I hadn't made some other mistake in braking or corner-entry judgment. Perhaps I had just blown it on that one particular lap and had driven too deeply. The professional in me wanted to think that the brake ghosts had made a timely appearance to bring me down a few notches. The realist in me understood that I might simply have messed up. Ultimately, it doesn't really matter. I was the guy behind the wheel when the car came to the track. I was the guy behind the wheel in the moments things went wrong. I was the guy behind the wheel who mowed a landing strip in the brambles with a Viper. I was the guy, no one else. The painful lesson to be learned was mine and mine alone. No one else was responsible. I was the guy.

Shortly after staff had begun arriving that following morning, I met with Dan, with Brian, and with my boss. Once I had provided the event play-by-play, there was little left for me to do except apologize for creating a mess for my personal friends, for the company, and for our friends at Dodge. I was responsible for letting them down. I was the guy behind the wheel. They all had their theories on what had happened. They all empathized with my situation and tried not to make it worse. Time would mostly heal those wounds in a positive way, but valuable lessons and durable scars remain.

In 2014, Admiral William H. McRaven delivered a memorable commencement address to the graduates of the University of Texas at Austin in which he shared applicable life lessons that he and his fellow sailors had extracted from their months of arduous SEAL training. His speech went viral. So inspirational was his speech that it was developed further and recently released by Admiral McRaven in a book entitled *Make Your Bed*. In both the speech and the book, Admiral McRaven describes an inescapable reality of SEAL training, the fact that, at one point or another during SEAL training, everyone became a "sugar cookie." If a trainee failed, even in the smallest of ways, or perhaps just found himself squarely in the crosshairs of a particularly irritated instructor, he would be forced to run fully clothed into the ocean, return immediately to the beach, and roll around in the soft sand to cover every inch and fill every nook. The look and effect was that of a sugar cookie, and the trainee would remain in this condition throughout the events and drills of the entire day. The lesson to trainees:

> Life is not always fair. Get over it and find
> a way to keep moving forward.

I was a sugar cookie with bite marks from a Viper. It was my time. I needed to take my lumps, get over it, and find a way to keep moving forward.

CHAPTER 8

LOVING ONE WOMAN AND LAPPING AMERICA

Lessons on Patience, Redemption, Marriage, and Starting a Family

WITH THE WINTER OF 1999–2000 CAME ANOTHER SNOW-TESTING campaign in the Upper Peninsula of Michigan and another family snowmobiling adventure based out of my hotel room. Dad, Shawn, and Shawn's boys were there. It was January 2000. We were playing ping-pong in the hotel's rec room. Out of the blue, Shawn informed me that Tekoa had been asking if I would be interested in reconnecting with her. He wanted to know if I was open to hearing from her. I would be delighted—overjoyed, in fact—but I didn't allow myself to respond that way. I certainly had *not* forgotten about her, but I had placed her carefully on the proverbial shelf, out of view, so that I could continue with my life and think fresh thoughts.

In that moment, my head was into my job and the visit from my family. I did not expect this topic. I did not see it coming. I remember stopping the ping-pong game abruptly, putting the paddle and ball on the table, focusing on what was being said, and asking Shawn some additional questions. I needed to understand the hows, the whys, and the whens of the situation. Did Tekoa recall that the ball was left clearly in *her* court to contact *me*? Satisfied with Shawn's answers to such questions, I looked to Dad. Dad's input was to be the deal maker or the deal breaker. That's God's honest truth. If Dad said, "Stay away from her," that would be it. Everything within me wanted to reconnect with Tekoa, but only if conditions were right, and only if Dad supported the idea.

"Spence, I know how much she meant to you in those days a year and a half ago and how disappointed you were to see her go. I think enough time has passed. I think you should give her another chance." *Amen!* Thank you, Dad!

Without showing the extent of my excitement, I explained to Shawn that I would indeed like to reconnect with her but that my stipulation remained. I needed to hear from her first. This family conversation alongside a ping-pong table in Michigan's Upper Peninsula didn't check that box. I wasn't going to require that she literally call me, but I was going to need some clear confirmation that she, too, wanted to reconnect with a purpose. Reconnecting had to be substantive, not merely a satisfaction of her curiosity as to what was new in my world. I had neither time for nor interest in something that was just friendly or casual.

Within a few days, Tekoa did communicate through Shawn that she wanted to reconnect in a meaningful way and that she would like for me to call her. I happily obliged. It was wonderful to hear her voice again and to know that there was hope for a deeper relationship. We made plans to see each other again as I was returning from Michigan to South Carolina on the evening of Friday, January 28, 2000.

Reconnecting with Tekoa was heavenly. Whatever fetters or concerns had confined her many months before were gone. It was as if time had stood still, not a day had passed, and we had never been apart. Leaving the story there for the moment and skipping well ahead, I'll tell you that we were married on Saturday, September 9, 2000, and remain happily married with three great kids, two psychotic pets, two goats, and so much more. We are richly blessed. I love Tekoa as deeply as a man can love a woman. I have my brother to thank for the connection and the reconnection, and my dad to thank for the wisdom to proceed.

Tekoa and I, together again in spring 2000

The year 2000 was a spectacular year. With the exception of damaging the ACL in my left knee in the first few days of January, it was mostly a year of redemption and success, Tekoa's and my reconnection, courtship, and marriage being the highest of the highlights. Following my reconnection with Tekoa on January 28, one might well imagine it was difficult for me to leave her and continue south on January 30. Doing so, however, did allow me to celebrate Bob's seventy-sixth birthday at his home on the evening of the thirtieth. I enjoyed the look of surprise on his face at my unexpected arrival, and I was excited to share my welcome relationship news with him. Bob was delighted for me and eager to welcome this special young lady into our lives and into our friendship circle.

My work at Michelin was going well. I had OE-account responsibility for Ford to be thankful for. Included in the Ford account was the Mustang, another red, white, and blue V8 muscle car for which I was developing considerable fondness. For many months, our tire-development team worked closely with Ford's Special Vehicle Team as they developed the SVT Cobra R. The Cobra R is a street-legal track version of the Mustang with production limited to three hundred units, making it legal for stock-racing classes. Cobra Rs in 2000 sat squarely in Vette and Viper territory. The Cobra R was a blast to drive, sounded as good as anything on the market, and had a great development team. John Coletti and his team at Ford SVT were savvy enough to engage Michelin's tire team closely in order to develop and fit the best possible tire to their car. They were also kind enough to include me personally in the development process. This relationship included invitations to drive in two separate twenty-four-hour endurance tests: one at Firebird Raceway in Arizona and another at MotorSport Ranch in Texas.

Life was good at the track. Scars from my earlier Viper crash were largely healed. Brian and I continued to push and challenge each other and our colleagues relentlessly, improving ourselves and team standards in the process. For several years, Brian and I had lobbied our bosses for the opportunity to represent Michelin in Brock Yates's One Lap of America race. Michelin was the title sponsor at the time, and One Lap was a prestigious, widely respected endurance event with a rich history dating back to the original 1971 Cannonball Baker Sea-to-Shining-Sea Memorial Trophy Dash. This race in the seventies ultimately inspired the 1981 film *The Cannonball Run*, starring Burt Reynolds.

With a dismissive response intended only to pacify, my boss suggested that if we could come up with a competitive ride, he would support our participation. He didn't believe we could come up with a competitive ride. He also really didn't think deeply about the nature of the two characters lobbying for the chance to race. His few words provided all the leash we needed.

I worked on my Ford colleagues, and Brian worked on his connections at Dodge. With little time to spare, Brian's work with Dodge bore fruit. One particular development manager at Dodge had enough spirit and risk tolerance that he had a well-used test Viper rescued from the crusher queue. He shipped the car to South Carolina with the clearest of instructions that we be careful. It was clear that he didn't want *anything* to go wrong. Perhaps he hadn't crossed every *t* or dotted every *i* in making this happen and was concerned about getting himself in a pickle if something did go wrong.

We cleared all the administrative hurdles at the eleventh hour and left our boss almost literally agape in slack-jawed amazement as we sorted and stuffed the last of our things into a borrowed, well-worn Viper before vanishing for a week—*paid*, thank you very much. Brian and I went racing in One Lap, and I was handed the opportunity to redeem and reinstate myself at the helm of a Viper. The day we left for the race was Tekoa's birthday, interestingly enough.

BRIAN AND I WITH OUR CRUSHER-QUEUE VIPER, ONE LAP 2000

It was a tough, competitive week. We covered more than four thousand miles and competed in nine separate events on five circuits against solid drivers with more powerful cars and more sophisticated equipment. It all came down to the final stage, on the final day of the week at GingerMan Raceway, outside South Haven, Michigan, on Saturday, May 13, 2000. It proved to be the closest finish up to that point in One Lap history, and it was our race to win or to lose, depending upon perspective.

Though we were down on horsepower, we had survived all week at or near the top of the 120-car field with consistent top-five performances. We had come into the final stage with a narrow lead but could easily lose it in these final three laps. Brian and I had rotated driving duties all week. In this final stage, I was the guy behind the wheel. This was an opportunity to write a new ending to my Viper story. My parents were there. My brother, Shawn, and his young son Austin were there. Brian's dad, Larry, had shadowed us all week, so he was there. Our friend Ryan was there. Most notably, Tekoa was there. Scores of other family, friends, and coworkers who had followed our progress throughout the week were also watching online as the stage was set for the final showdown. This was more than just Spencer and Brian vs. the field in the closest race in One Lap history. This was also Spencer vs. Viper, round two.

I was the first car out on the pace lap, followed shortly by our nearest two competitors. Sean Roe, in a Hennessey Viper sporting two hundred horsepower more than our car, was first in line behind me. As I slowly made my way around the pace lap, getting my car up to temperature and visualizing each move at each position, Sean played his best mind games. He was sweeping back and forth at my rear bumper, filling one mirror then the next, hoping it would break my concentration. As the starting line approached, and the flag dropped, I began carefully executing the plan I had visualized in my mind's eye. Some fifteen seconds later, Sean Roe got the green flag. Then, another fifteen seconds later, Paul Gerrard got the green flag in his RENNtech Mercedes. After the second of three laps was complete, it became clear to me that Sean's swagger and aggression had come to naught. In his drive to catch me, he spun out somewhere behind me and fell out of view and out of contention. Paul and his Mercedes also appeared to be losing ground. I just had to execute through the final lap. This time there would be no mistakes, no ghosts, and no doubt. By the grace of God, this time, I've got this.

As I took the checker, I was fairly confident we had reason to celebrate, but I couldn't yet be certain. Remember, all of this is based on elapsed time and points accumulated over the course of an entire week, so I had no way of knowing for sure so soon from inside the car. The look on Brian's whole person as I rolled back toward the paddock told the story. He made no attempt to limit his excitement. It remains to date the most excited I have ever seen Brian. Together, we had done it! This pair of Michelin rookies in a whipped-out, borrowed test Viper had outlasted and outrun the field. We won!

As I was still cruising from the pits toward the paddock, Brian came running. We clenched hands through the driver's window in absolute, unrestrained joy. He hopped onto the hood, pounding on the roof and hollering in excitement as I rolled toward our space, farther on in the paddock. Fifty yards from our space in the paddock, on a pristine expanse of black asphalt, the crowd cleared just enough. I told Brian to hold on. I lit and boiled the rear tires we had so carefully cared for and preserved all week. For the next fifteen seconds, and more than forty yards, we smoked and slithered our way in and out of the few spectators and parked cars that punctuated our path, coming to rest as intended in the paddock position adjacent to my parents' motor home. The long, flowing dual black patches, the lingering smoke, and the unmistakable smell of burning rubber paid proper tribute to the exhausted yet unflappable silver Viper that had carried us to victory. What an event! What an outcome!

BRIAN AND I, ONE LAP CHAMPS, 2000

Though I sincerely regret and humbly admit that I don't recall his name, I am most thankful to that courageous manager from Dodge who had the fortitude and the faith to put his name on the line for Brian and me. To him and to all who supported us, I am very grateful. We appreciated the support more than you may know. It is worth mentioning that the manager from Dodge who took a chance on us was praised for his actions. Our victory was celebrated widely within their corporate walls. Our beloved Viper did not go to the crusher after all, at least not right away. Instead, it went on tour. Dodge didn't even want the stickers removed or the grit and grime from the track wiped away. Just as it was from the finish, the car was included in Dodge motorsports tours and displays. Our success made for great Dodge motorsports press. Lessons and reminders to self from this experience and the one to follow:

> Go out on a limb for the most succulent fruit once in a while. Take chances on good-willed folks every now and again. Failure doesn't have to be final.

Only a few months later, life got even better. Tekoa and I were married at Saint Mary's Catholic Church, my family's home church in Dunnington, Indiana, on a beautiful Saturday afternoon, September 9, 2000. It would have been the sixty-ninth wedding anniversary of my grandparents on Dad's side had Grandma not passed away several years prior. Grandpa was there to celebrate with us. Dad was in our wedding party, and Shawn was my best man. Brian, Brian's parents, my good friend Matt, and several of my fraternity brothers also attended. Ken from GM and his wife, Tricia, were also able to celebrate with us. Bob was not able to join us physically, but he was certainly present in spirit.

Beyond the fact that it was our wedding day, and I was marrying the woman of my dreams, there was a particularly memorable automotive element worthy of note: the getaway. Remember Ford's SVT Cobra R and the great team of folks I worked with on that project? With the right requests from the right Michelin people to the right Ford people, a Cobra R had become available for our wedding. Unbelievable as that may sound, management of Ford's SVT team allowed my friend Dave, the Michelin account manager responsible for the Ford account at that time, to take one of the SVT Cobra R test cars for the weekend. Dave was already planning to attend our wedding, so, naturally, he just drove the Cobra R instead of his own vehicle from Dearborn to our humble church in rural Indiana.

As I have written, edited, and reread this paragraph about the Cobra R many times, now, more than twenty years after it became part of our special day, I'm surprised ever more that it actually came to be. Every day it seems our society becomes more and more litigious. Companies, particularly large ones, depart less and less from their strict rules and regulations designed to protect them from fools and lawsuits. Fewer and fewer people in positions of power are willing to interpret rules loosely or take chances. There was almost nothing of value for Ford in this extension of courtesy beyond goodwill. It wasn't as if they were loaning us a Cobra R for One Lap of America, where there was an opportunity to gain publicity or notch another win on their corporate belt. Instead, Mr. Coletti allowed one of their precious test cars to accumulate many miles and be exposed to additional risk on the public roadways for an entire weekend simply as a nice gesture to an extended member of his team. It was a kind extension of goodwill and a supremely cool move. John Coletti is that sort of guy. Bold, gutsy, a bit brazen—he's the sort of guy who gets things done, sometimes things that don't make sense to the masses. John would also have enjoyed and approved of the getaway burnout.

Though usage of the Cobra R had been agreed upon and planned well in advance, until Dave and his wife arrived safely, I would have a small measure of concern as to what was actually going to be available for our getaway. True to form, Dave managed his part perfectly. He showed up at my parents' house with an angry red Cobra R almost three hours before the wedding, plenty of time for me to wash and shake down the car. Our beautiful car, now clean and shiny, had a slight problem. This test car had arrived with baggage from a rough life. The clutch was on its last leg. My test launch for a burnout resulted in lots of clutch slip and almost no wheelspin. These are not the ingredients for a great getaway. Our solution was liberal usage of Armor All, not on the sidewall but on the tread.

Shawn, being best man and an avid car guy, had well in hand the task of prepping the car for burnout. Our wedding was everything we could hope for, and the getaway came off without a hitch. I informed the photographer ahead of time of my plans to let the smoke roll from a stationary burnout so that he could get a proper picture of the kiss from the front of the car, then from the back as we smoked slowly past. The Armor All did its job.

"R" wedding getaway, September 9, 2000

The clutch hooked more happily than the tires, and, within a few revolutions, tire smoke was billowing. The kiss, the pictures, the prolonged burnout rolling slowly in front of the crowd—it all completed a perfect ceremony thanks first to my lovely bride, then to my friends at Ford SVT, my friend Dave, my brother, Shawn, and a liberal application of Armor All. Thank you, one and all.

Early days of marriage are supposed to be special. Ours were. We enjoyed each other immensely, spending evenings at home together, working out, going for jogs, catching new episodes of *Friends*, and celebrating church with Bob. We took strolls through Clemson's botanical gardens, went on motorcycle trips into the mountains, and enjoyed weekend getaways to Charleston. We enjoyed it all, together. Tekoa and I both have many fond memories of those years.

One of our most vivid and cherished memories was the moment Tekoa shared with me that she was pregnant. We had been married fourteen or fifteen months when we began trying to conceive a child. Our original plan was to enjoy two full years together, just us, really enjoying and getting to know one another before introducing a newborn into our family. We accelerated that plan slightly based on Tekoa's desire to get moving and her statement "I know my body. It may take several months once we start trying." Funny girl.

A little more than one month later, Tekoa was standing on the landing of a small porch at the back of our little A-frame in the woods. Our young beagle, Indy, was at her feet. As if she were up to something, Tekoa drew my attention up to her, away from whatever it was I had been working on under my carport. She radiated with an all-encompassing glow of contained glee. She handed me the stick from a pregnancy test and waited for my reaction: *positive*. I set the stick on the edge of the porch, and, by the time I reached up to catch her in a celebratory embrace, two things happened. First, she had already begun simultaneously laughing and crying tears of joy as she met my embrace. Second, our jealous dog grabbed the pregnancy stick and ran off into the woods. Our pregnancy celebration was nipped in the bud by a belligerent beagle who would have nothing of her affections being redirected to a helpless infant.

In those days, our lives were filled with excitement, anticipation, and hope. There was little about which to worry. We had a great marriage, good health, adequate money, and plenty of marketable skills. We had each other, and we were happy. Tekoa quickly became comfortable in South Carolina. She made many new friends, she developed a love of exercise and instruction at the local YMCA, and she was able to pursue some passions she had previously presumed unobtainable, including working part-time as a technician in a local animal clinic to feed her love and concern for animals.

My work was also going well. Tekoa and I were formulating plans for where we would like to take our lives next. I was at the top of my driving game. Brian and I went on to capture our second One Lap of America victory in 2001, once again in a Viper. Our racing interests were advancing, folks were taking notice, and we started picking up a few notable sponsors along the way. In the spring of 2002, we opted to compete *against* one another for a third One Lap of America victory in hopes of drumming up even more publicity for both of us.

I was hired by a dentist from New England to drive his Mercedes CLK60, heavily modified by German tuner RENNtech. Brian was once again driving a Viper provided by Dodge. By this time, neither of us was squeaking by with crusher-queue equipment. Both his car and mine were properly outfitted. They were highly potent track cars capable of winning the event without massive doses of luck or the misfortune of others. Our rivalry in the making was short-lived, however.

My car, competitive though it was in the first two laps of the very first event, blew a hole in its engine block before the end of the third lap. Though the oil temperature gauge was previously believed to be defective, we came to understand that it was indeed working properly. When the car was driven hard, oil temperature skyrocketed, and catastrophic failure was inevitable. The engine block ventilated only two short corners from the finish line, sending oil everywhere before I could get off the track. I hobbled across the finish line, using my wipers to clear enough oil from my windshield to keep from hitting anything. The car was fast and would have been a real threat to win the overall event had we been able to keep it together. Even limping across the line at the end of the third lap, its total elapsed time was still fast enough for a third-place finish in that specific round. Rather than winning, though, it harmlessly caught fire a few hundred yards past the finish line.

Brian and his Viper completed the week, winning a third straight One Lap of America title. Congratulations on your third straight, Brian!

CHAPTER 9

JOHN LINGENFELTER

Lessons on Power, Preparation, Expectations, and Humble Support

SINCE STARTING WITH MICHELIN IN 1995 THROUGH AT LEAST 2000, I HAD stayed in contact with my friend Ken from GM. We snowmobiled together in Michigan and Wyoming, and Ken had come to know my dad on a few of these snowmobiling trips. We talked occasionally of what we were doing in our respective careers and of my racing. Ken celebrated my progress at Michelin and our Viper victories in One Lap, and he was at our wedding cheering and championing me as the smoke rolled from the rear tires of Ford's Cobra R. The time was past due for me to reconnect with GM and Corvettes in some way. That day came in 2002 by way of the man, the myth, the legend—John Lingenfelter. I am honored and thankful to have had the opportunity to come to know and work with John and his team.

I fondly recall the first time I met John Lingenfelter for a test session in early 2002. He reminded me of my dad. John was a towering figure in the performance industry but a relatively short, stocky, ordinary-looking fellow standing there in the paddock at Putnam Park. He wore blue jeans and a simple shirt. He had salt-and-pepper hair, thick workman's hands with a mechanical grip, and a welcoming smile. John would have blended into a collection of farmers around the sunrise coffee table like a chameleon. It seems unlikely, though, that he would be found there, at least not for long. More likely, he would be in his shop tinkering with another notion to make more horsepower.

There in the paddock at Putnam Park, John didn't ask for my credentials or try to explain anything I already knew about driving. John was an excellent drag racer in his own right. He wasn't distracted by risk or damage or contracts. He knew of me from others within Michelin who spoke for my competence. That was enough for him. We reviewed a few details of the boosted beasts he had brought to the track but didn't linger or let technical discussion get in the way of the job at hand. John was as eager as I to bring them to life and start assessing and improving their performance.

Perform they did. With somewhere around seven hundred horsepower from twin-turbocharged V8s, they were automotive weapons like nothing I had experienced up to that point. We tested two vehicles that day. The first and the fastest was a canary yellow Corvette with a big-block 427 fed by two turbochargers. The second was a fire-engine red GMC S-15 Sonoma pickup truck with a twin-turbo small-block 350 and an all-wheel drive system grafted from a Yukon Denali. Other than slightly lowered stances, nominally oversized wheels and tires, purposeful rumbles at idle, and inconspicuous LPE badging, the average passerby might never have taken note of these vehicles, let alone appreciated the excellence beneath their skins.

The Vette was brutally fast. Below boost, the car felt visceral and poised, patiently burbling along in strained comfort, just waiting for a target and space to release. On boost, however, this Vette offered all the excitement of mouthing a kazoo and strapping oneself to a bottle rocket with a steering wheel. Automotive exhilaration doesn't get much more intense, at least not on the street. Providing similar excitement, but in a vastly different package, was the S-15 Sonoma. With its factory belts and flat factory bench seat, the Sonoma experience was more akin to saddling up to a love-deprived, slobbering Brahman bull. You sat atop a slick, velvety perch inches from a pounding heart of mechanical attitude with instantaneous reactions but little poise. The launch strategy for the Sonoma according to John was "Bring it up to 2500, then mat it." Throttle response and emergence from the gate was instantaneous. Until that day at Putnam Park, I don't ever recall having previously laughed out loud inside a car from pure joy and the experience of lunacy. John's creations were something to behold.

A few months later, in the summer of 2002, John, his team, and I were together again at Michigan International Speedway at the second-ever Car and Driver Supercar Challenge to put these same machines to the test against the best equipment other tuners had brought to the event. Included in this mix was John Hennessey with one of his venomous Vipers, my buddy Brian handling its driving duties.

The event was designed like an overgrown, high-speed autocross, where lowest total elapsed time wins. Competing vehicles took to the track one at a time. The clock and data-acquisition equipment triggered with the first movement of the vehicle from the starting line on the back straightaway between Turn 2 and Turn 3. From this starting point, there was plenty of straight-line distance available to complete a full quarter-mile pass before throwing out the anchor and drifting down into a simple road course in the infield ahead of Turn 3. Upon completion of the infield road course, vehicles bounded back out onto the oval just before Turn 3 and raced toward a cone chicane set low in the middle of banking between Turns 3 and 4. The chicane was intended to limit corner speed on the banking. Once through the chicane, machines accelerated with full fury onto Turn 4 and the front straightaway. The mission in this final sector was to reach 150 mph as quickly as possible, followed immediately by the hardest possible braking down to 0 mph.

Sector times and several channels of data were collected, but, ultimately, all that mattered for the overall win was which vehicle posted the lowest overall elapsed time from 0 mph at the starting line back down to 0 mph somewhere on the front straight. Each driver had five laps to lay down his quickest lap. Just like an autocross, each cone knocked down or out of position added two seconds to the elapsed time. Given the highly competitive field, hitting a cone was a death sentence for that lap.

There was also no opportunity for test runs. You got five laps. That's it. Learn fast and make them count.

Once our vehicles had been unloaded and prepped, I took a few moments to talk with John and the LPE team about anything that might have changed since the test session at Putnam Park a few months prior. Was there anything that might affect my job behind the wheel? John calmly and matter-of-factly explained that his team had changed the motor in the Sonoma from the 350 cu. in. twin-turbo that we had tested at Putnam to a larger 427 cu. in. twin-turbo for this event. John barely looked up. "We dialed the boost back a little to compensate for the added displacement. You shouldn't notice much difference." As the only truck in the event, the Sonoma might have drawn extra attention, but it didn't. Spectators were drawn instead to visual flash and presumptions of speed based on styling or a certain manufacturer's logo. Slipping in under the radar was fine with John. He didn't need the flash. His character was quiet and confident. John was not one to draw much attention to himself or his products beyond the attention each attracted by its performance and attention to detail.

Actions speak louder than words.

Other than the LPE team, my buddy Brian, and the technicians manning the equipment at the starting line, not many folks even recognized that I had brought the Sonoma into position. The yawns were visible, and the indifference almost palpable.

"What comes after this little truck thing?" the body language of the audience seemed to inquire.

With 2500 rpm stabilized on the tach and the thumbs-up from the technical folks, I matted it. An even bigger, more instantaneous, more agitated response rocketed the angry red bull from the line, its chassis distinctly twisted by the motor's torque. The shift of the automatic transmission from first gear to second at nearly 50 mph was hard enough to send a shudder through the entire truck as all four tires lost and sought traction once again, and the truck sidestepped slightly down the banking. If the test truck from Putnam Park had felt like an agitated Brahman bull, this bigger motor sent it several steps back in history to its bigger, nastier, harder-working, less domesticated roots. This was one angry-fast little pickup.

So, how fast was this boosted Sonoma, you ask? Well, it sprinted from 0 to 60 mph in 2.8 seconds and completed the quarter mile in 10.6 seconds at 135 mph. For perspective—and roughly $350,000—one can buy a brand-new 2021 McLaren 720S that runs nearly identical numbers.

The 720S is arguably one of the fastest, most well-rounded exotic cars currently available for less than a million dollars. Yes, John Lingenfelter's Sonoma was fast.

A Sonoma victory wasn't meant to be, however. As fast as the Sonoma was in a straight line, the lateral loading under power entering the infield was high enough for long enough that the transmission waved a white flag. It was among the first vehicles loaded back onto the trailer. It is truly a shame that our day with the Sonoma had to end so soon. That nasty little truck had much more to show than just straight-line prowess, which it had in spades. With only one pass through only one sector, the Sonoma's time and speed through that sector stood all day as the fastest of the group—by considerable margin.

Following that unfortunate start with the Sonoma, the outlook improved considerably for our Corvette. It became clear early that our Lingenfelter Vette; Hennessey's Viper, driven by Brian; and a lightning-quick, all-wheel drive Porsche 911, driven by Paul Gerrard, were the combinations to beat for fast time of the day. After three laps, our Vette was at the front of the pack, but I hadn't yet put everything together for my fastest clean lap. There was a cone or two here and there, and I overshot the 150 mph target by a couple of miles per hour on each lap. While there is no imposed penalty for overshooting 150 mph, doing so is a big problem. It takes that much more *time* to brake back down to 0 mph. Victory would have to be earned in this group. We were in front, but the gap was closing. I had to tidy things up and put it all together.

John was disappointed that the Sonoma was out so soon. He had high hopes that the Vette could help him save some face with an overall win. He voiced neither of those thoughts, but they were clear in his demeanor. My third run, imperfect though it was, was the fastest of the group so far. John and I both knew I hadn't yet found all there was to find. John softly suggested,

"You might try running with your windows up."

John didn't force, demand, or belittle with his suggestion. He simply prompted my thinking to explore new ideas. Perhaps the benefits of having my windows up at higher speeds and under hard acceleration might outweigh known drawbacks. He was after those fractions of a second that can make the difference between a win and a loss.

Paul in the Porsche, with its all-wheel drive benefits at launch and in the tight road course, closed the gap to almost nothing with his fourth lap. I tried John's approach with the windows up on my fourth lap, which was better yet, but still not nearly all I could muster. On this fourth lap, I also hit yet another cone. On Paul's fifth and final lap, he found more time with his 911 in a cone-free run and precariously held the fastest time of the day by a small margin. *I was not pleased.* The pressure was on to bring everything together cleanly on my fifth and final lap.

I knew the car and I both had capacity yet untapped to emerge victorious for John and his team. I just had to extract it. Not once did John express any disappointment or dissatisfaction with me, not even with his body language. Instead, with my last remaining lap approaching, John strolled over next to me casually, shoulder to shoulder, hands half in, half out of his jeans pockets. He shared the distant gaze I maintained on the track. I was visualizing every step, every visual reference, every shift point. Step-by-step around the track, I needed to execute perfectly. Without breaking my concentration, attempting only to offer words of encouragement, John said quietly but clearly,

"I hired you for good reason. I have confidence in you. Just relax. Do what you know needs to be done."

He shared my distant gaze and never even looked at me. Rather, he gave a supportive pat on my shoulder with one of those experienced-mechanic hands, then turned and walked confidently away. More timely and helpful words may never have been provided.

The time had come to deliver—showtime. *Windows up, launch good, shifts good, quarter mile good, road course good, exit onto Turn 3 good. Now, do* not *downshift to second for the chicane. Stay in third and focus entirely on maximum clean speed through the chicane. The chicane* must *be clean. Then, release the motor. Let 'er eat.* When I exited the last gate of the chicane in third gear, I glanced for a split second in my rearview mirror as the LPE rocket motor came on boost. Brief though it was, my glance suggested the pass was clean, and the full fury of 427 LPE-boosted cubic inches was not to be denied. I knew we had our event-winning run if I could just nail 150 mph precisely and get to the brakes immediately.

One of the challenges with this seemingly simple task was that this car accelerated so fast, even above 140 mph, that the digital speedometer couldn't keep up. It was rapidly updating the display in chunks of three or four miles per hour at a time. I had to quickly calibrate the chunks of displayed speed to the actual ground speed recorded by the onboard equipment. The display on my speedometer and the speed recorded by the data-acquisition equipment were not exactly the same. There had been a slight offset all day. If you undershot and didn't reach 150 mph, the run would be considered a DNF (did not finish), null and void, a total waste. If you overshot by much at all, the extra time required to get back down to 0 mph would likely take you out of contention for the title.

I went to 100% brake as the last chunk of speed displayed 148 mph. Based on results from previous runs, I figured that should put us at about 151 mph actual ground speed as recorded by the data-acquisition equipment.

Decelerating hard at full ABS but still well over 100 mph, I immediately pushed "Express Down" for both windows. The windows shook with considerable violence as they descended, and the cabin boomed like a bass drum with the pressure change. I also tried to open my door against the rushing wind for maximum air resistance.

Coming to a halt perhaps forty or fifty yards short of my previous best run, I was hopeful it was enough. I made my way back to the paddock with restrained confidence and excitement that we had just brought home a trophy for John and his team with that final pass. We had!

As I pulled into the paddock, left hand out the window delivering a few gentle pats of appreciation to the roof of that awesome, predatory Vette, John and the crowd acknowledged our run kindly with raised fists and clapping hands. We had delivered our best. It was all we could do. The smile on John's face, the ecstatic expressions on the faces of the LPE team members, and the looks of disbelief on the faces of almost everyone else are something I wish I could have bottled up to save for tougher days.

John had hired me to do a job I was qualified to do. He had entrusted me with much and expected much. Notice I said that he *expected* much, not that he wanted, intended, or demanded much. Wants and intentions show up in discussions.

Expectations show up in actions.

John expected much. He had prepared his vehicles and his team. He had hired someone he expected to perform at a high level. He had encouraged and helped that guy fine-tune his own performance to extract everything that was available to extract. Together we earned a title that easily could have gone to someone else.

As the ceremonies to close the event approached, a member of John's team handed me a Lingenfelter Performance Engineering shirt in anticipation of any pictures or comments. Upon being presented with two trophies—one for biggest and earliest breakdown and one for the overall win—John donned a contented smile and spoke a few appreciative, simple words into the microphone. He neither made excuses for the early demise of the Sonoma nor gloated over our win with the Vette, but he did thank me for the positive contribution I had made toward the team's win. John was that kind of a guy.

In the years to come, I would drive other ultraimpressive LPE creations, at one point going more than 226 mph in a standing mile. But, I never again drove with as much success and joy as I had at that first event with John back in the summer of 2002. John died on Christmas Day 2003 as a result of complications from surgery. He had crashed in a drag-racing event in California in October 2002 and never fully recovered. I heard somewhere that, at one point, after having come briefly out of a coma, John shared with his team some of the new horsepower ideas he was constructing during his quiet time in the coma. I don't know if it is true, but it sounds about right. I am grateful for the opportunity to have come to know and work with John. Whether he knew it or not, through just a few interactions over the course of a handful of months, John had impressed upon me his lessons about preparation, humility, teamwork, patience, trust, and support, to name but a few.

JOHN LINGENFELTER WITH SUPERCAR CHALLENGE TROPHIES, 2002

Rest in peace, John. It was a pleasure getting to know you. You are certainly appreciated and missed.

CHAPTER 10

DEVELOPING ON DIXON ROAD

Lessons on Mom's Wisdom, Simple Generosity,
Roadside Pepper, and Landscape Salt

BACK IN SOUTH CAROLINA, OUR FAMILY AND OUR HOMESTEAD WERE developing, quite literally. As Tekoa's pregnancy progressed, we spent time researching and inspecting real estate. We leveraged Dad's experience as a real-estate broker from afar. We missed out on a couple of opportunities that were not meant to be. Eventually, we purchased a country parcel on the outskirts of Laurens.

The property had been an active farm years before with a small brick home, remnants of other quarters, and a few dilapidated farm structures. It was a picturesque fourteen-acre property with desirable natural topography overlooking rolling hayfields and woods. It was conveniently located and had more than a thousand feet of quality road frontage on two sides. We had the land surveyed and replotted, then sold the original brick home and three acres that went naturally with it. We kept the remaining eleven acres to improve and build a home for our new family. Tekoa and I had great fun planning our new home. We imagined its placement and orientation, along with the views from a large bay window in the second-floor master bedroom overlooking the fields and forest. We spent many evenings and weekends in the summer of 2002 clearing overgrown areas, laying out enclosures for animals, removing defunct farm structures that we could raze by hand, and grooming the area that was to become our front yard.

On one particular weekend, the work became a family affair. Mom and Dad traveled down, along with Shawn and his boys. I rented a small dozer and a backhoe in order to clean up the remaining buildings and patches that were not practical to manage by hand. Dad was in his element, running equipment as he did back in his early days with the Soil Conservation Service. Shawn, too, is a skilled equipment operator. He was busy bringing down unwanted trees, managing burn piles, and burying rocks and miscellaneous debris. Mom was a distant supervisor, keeping the younger boys out of harm's way and ensuring her crew had adequate food and drink. By the end of our weekend, it looked like a different property, restored and ready for a fresh start. Construction and finishing of our new home was nearing completion, as well. Good thing; we were close enough to Tekoa's due date that child number one could arrive any time. With the help of our friends Matt and Tracy, we moved into our home in late July, less than two weeks before Sawyer's birth.

Sawyer Paul Geswein was born in August 2002. Giving him the middle name *Paul*, after my dad, was a gesture of respect and appreciation. We had no idea at the time what a bond these men from totally different generations would form in the years to come.

From late 2002 through 2004, my parents made numerous trips between Indiana and South Carolina. The first of these trips came just days after Sawyer's birth. It was a welcome and educational visit, to say the least.

It bears repeating that parenting is difficult. There is no manual. Every child is different, and new parents generally have no clue. We were no different, mostly clueless. The first child can present considerable challenge. Learning the ropes often involves doing something wrong and suffering the consequences. While we were still at the hospital with nurses to help and nurseries to muffle the noise, parenting seemed easy—no big deal. Once we were home, reality hit! The feedings, the diaper changes, the constant crying, and the lack of sleep converged. In those earliest days at the house, Sawyer just wouldn't sleep. His crying was constant. It was incessant. We questioned our sanity and laughingly wondered if there was a way to put him back. We felt as though we were suffering the consequences of some egregious parenting error. Until Mom and Dad showed up, we had no idea what.

DAD AND SAWYER PAUL, 2002

Apparently, the American Academy of Pediatrics, and likely others, concluded in those years that newborns sleeping on their backs are safer than newborns sleeping on their stomachs. That may well be true. Truer still is the fact that a sleeping baby and a rested family are both happier and healthier than the exhausted versions of themselves. Mom, mother of three and a registered nurse, had enough maternal instinct, experience, and wisdom to know better. She immediately put Mr. Sawyer on his stomach. Already in motion, she said, "Oh Honey, just put him on his tummy. He'll be fine. He's just uncomfortable."

This action and guidance came from a woman who worried endlessly about many, many things. A risk-taker Mom was not. Within minutes, Sawyer was out. One small step for Sawyer and Grandma, one giant leap for parenthood and sanity in the Geswein home. Thanks, Mom. Mom's wise but unspoken lesson might run something along these lines: There is nothing wrong with considering new ideas, trying new methods, and seeking additional enlightenment. Experience, too, can be a great teacher. The fact that some gadget, practice, or theory is new doesn't necessarily make it better. You are not required to possess or adopt all things new.

We can learn a lot from our parents and others with "fruit on the tree." Just do your best with logic and abundant love.

Bob was thrilled with the expansion of our family. One of Sawyer's first birthday gifts was $1000 from Bob. Is $1000 from Bob starting to sound like a recurring theme? A curious thing is a gift such as this, to be appreciated more deeply than the face value of the currency. I never asked why Bob had felt compelled to give such a generous gift at Sawyer's birth. I could have asked him over the years since then, but I didn't do that, either. I believe it is better just to appreciate the gift, to contemplate its intent, and to savor the friendship. I think Bob's gift was simply the bountiful love and generosity of a true friend, just like his previous gifts. Each gift communicated its own message. This one silently trumpeted forth, "Welcome, young man! I'm glad you are here. I'm proud of your parents. I'm hopeful for your future, and I can't wait to include you in this treasured friendship. I'm just a happy friend. Put this little gift somewhere smart and safe. You will appreciate it later, and I'll enjoy a smile. Welcome with love and prayers, my boy, welcome."

I can almost hear Bob saying such words. The apostle Paul, in his careful wording, had it right when he wrote to Timothy, "The love of money is the root of all evils" (I Timothy 6:10). Money is a tool. It has no moral underpinnings. It can be used for good or for evil, depending upon the spirit of the one who handles it. Bob's attitude and behavior around money provided a great example. It was just money. He was comfortable. He had plenty.

Share what you have and love much.
That's it, simple.

BOB AND SAWYER, 2004

We appreciated his gifts, each of them, and we love Bob and his spirit. I hope to be such a friend, such a selfless and faithful manager of God's resources. Thank you, Bob.

Dad and I were working on something each time he and Mom came down for a visit. Masonry work, fencing, pouring concrete, seeding grass—you name it, we were getting it done. As I reflect on those days, I imagine it must have brought a measure of pride to my dad to see productive fruit from his many hours of trying to instill work ethic and teach practical skills. No longer did Dad always have to be the leader. A shift was finally beginning to take place. I knew what to do, I knew how to do it, and I developed a level of confidence and leadership that allowed me to work with Dad as his equal rather than forever his apprentice.

As good as that feels as the adult child, I'm certain it felt better for Dad. I know this to be true because today, in our own family, Tekoa and I are beginning to see this same sort of confidence and independence in our children as they move toward the edges of our figurative nest. This is true not only as it relates to work but also as it relates to life, faith, and community. We have every reason to believe that soon they will soar to new heights of their own choosing. Shared interests, shared goals, two men working together on productive projects—Dad and I were our own production team. Those were really good times with my dad. I cherish them.

In our new home, with our growing family, we made acquaintances and formed friendships with several folks and many dogs along our peaceful dead-end country road. My usage of terms here is careful and deliberate. On the acquaintances side were a pair of curmudgeons who were not fond of the young Yankees who had moved in. We had changed the landscape and shined light on conditions along the road needing improvement. Their properties and their persons were disheveled and unwelcoming. At one such property, a group of as many as twenty foul-tempered, mangy dogs were fed and watered but unmanaged. They were left alone to hassle passersby under the guise of protecting a deteriorating homeplace. There is no need to list names or make this paragraph any longer than it needs to be. Let's just say these folks were the roadside pepper. Their number was small.

Thankfully, at the saline end of the spectrum were folks greater in number and far greater in personal constitution, folks like our good friend Charles and each of his kin who lived along our road. There were great folks such as King and Augusta Dixon, mighty pillars of the community, from whom the road got its name. Each of these fine, upstanding Southern folks would give you the shirt off his back and all the time you needed over a glass of sweet tea to discuss whatever you might like to discuss. Their places were neat and tidy, and their faith and pride strong. Their speech was without vulgarity, vanity, or excuse, and their language drawn not to river-bottom colloquialism but instead to classy Southern style. Charles, King, Augusta, and others are salt-of-the-earth people who welcomed us as their own and made our stay on Dixon Road special. Finally, there was one big, black, beloved dog not to be forgotten: Lester.

"Associate yourself with men of good quality
if you esteem your own reputation; for 'tis
better to be alone than in bad company."

—George Washington

Tekoa and I have many great memories of our time on Dixon Road. A few deeper reflections on its people "of good quality" are worth sharing.

King and his wife, Augusta, are exemplary people. She is a proper Southern lady full of care, dignity, poise, and grace. He is a hardworking, decorated US Marine and University of South Carolina football legend. They are clean-living Christian people who have raised a great family together and have served their country and their community faithfully. They are examples of service and a marriage done well.

The time I first met King Dixon, I was unaware of all his accolades and decoration. I knew that he was a sturdy Southern gentleman known to be helpful in many regards. In the past, King and Charles had often shared the task of mowing the roadside of our newly acquired property. No one else previously had been eager to do it, and it needed to be done. King and Charles were the sorts who would get it done for the benefit of everyone on the road.

One day, upon hearing the sound of King's mower and seeing the dirt cloud from a particularly troublesome area to mow, I hustled down to the roadside to catch up with King. He shut his mower down and listened with a pleasant smile on his face as I introduced myself, thanked him (and Charles) for their past service on this property, and kindly asked him to skip my property from this point forward since I intended to manicure it the best I could in the future with a finish mower. King happily obliged, restarted his tractor, lifted his mower, cruised on down the road past the edge of our property, and resumed his mowing of the roadside for other residents en route back to his home, further down the road. I think King and I came to appreciate and understand each other reasonably well with that first meeting.

Respectful words, kind gestures, and goodwill delivered in the right spirit can accomplish a great deal.

I don't recall the details of my first encounter with Augusta, but I am certain it was positive and encouraging. I have nothing but respect for this wonderfully kind, sophisticated Southern lady. Augusta has nary a foul word to speak of anyone and nothing but faithful support of her husband and others. Augusta lives the principle my father so often verbalized:

"If you don't have anything nice to say, don't say anything at all." On one particular occasion, Tekoa had the opportunity to witness firsthand Augusta's kindness, maternal instinct, and rapid response.

ENJOYING A VISIT WITH KING AND AUGUSTA, 2004

Young Sawyer had managed to contort his little arm into a precarious and painful position between the thick wooden bars of his baby crib. He was unable to extract it on his own and was crying the pathetic cry of a youngster stuck and scared. As Tekoa's moments passed without success at extracting Sawyer's arm, she decided to call Ms. Augusta. In a flash, Augusta was on the scene with tools ranging from dish soap to a copious quantity of butter. In the three minutes it might have taken Augusta to arrive, Tekoa and Sawyer managed to escape. Had he still been ensnared, Augusta would have been more than prepared.

Tekoa and I so fondly recall sitting peacefully with King and Augusta on many occasions, taking in the sounds of nature and the trickling of their water garden as we enjoyed refreshment, fellowship, and engaging conversation.

SAWYER AND I WITH CHARLES, 2004

Charles is the Good Samaritan to everyone. He is a very devout, very kindly, very capable Southern gentleman. His home, his property, his priorities, and his person are always in good order, and he is always ready to be of assistance. Charles is one neighbor in particular I wish I had made the effort to know and to appreciate more fully while we lived on Dixon Road. He is always interested in others first, himself second. I recall numerous occasions as I was working various property or building projects when Charles would stop over. He would praise my progress and go out of his way to notice and comment on some particular design or construction technique I used that he really liked. He always asked if I needed his help or if I needed to borrow anything. I was too young, too foolish, and too self-absorbed to appreciate Charles as I should have. From this simple man, there is much to learn and admire. Toward the end of our days on Dixon Road, the quality and depth of his character would be revealed in an undeniable way. By then, sadly, the time to take full advantage of his mentorship had expired.

Jogging, speed walking, or simply strolling along, exchanging greetings with passing neighbors—such were our experiences and memories on Dixon Road. These experiences were seldom enjoyed without the company of good ole Lester, the big, black, loyal, rough-and-tumble canine master of the road. My reflections would be incomplete if I failed to express gratitude, like a scratch behind the ear, to this faithful friend. Like my beloved dog Duke from childhood, Lester was the canine version of Dad and other men whose lessons I've been sharing. Lester was a stud.

Lester made it his mission in life to accompany travelers and ensure safe passage past the road's mangy pack and other threats. No matter where Lester was along this road of more than one mile, it seemed he magically appeared mere moments before his service was required. He lumbered happily alongside, between you and trouble. Lester would not leave your side except to mark his turf and confront offenders. He did both regularly.

TEKOA AND GOOD OLE LESTER ON OUR FRONT PORCH, CIRCA 2003

The scenario was predictable. The pack of mangy thugs would taunt, harass, and inch closer until Lester had had his fill. Lester would advance ten or fifteen yards toward the threat, providing distance and cover to his pedestrians. Within moments, the brawl would begin. At times it was difficult to even see Lester in the mass of hair, teeth, claws, and dust. There would be deep sounds of effort and justice from Lester mixed with higher-frequency yelps and cries of surrender from the cowards. One by one they would retreat. Standing alone, unchallenged, Lester would turn to saunter happily back to our sides as if nothing had happened, rejoining our stroll with renewed peace and plenty of space.

He was usually missing small tufts of hair and bleeding harmlessly from cuts to his head and mouth, but the blood and saliva flipping from his gray tongue as he pranced victoriously was his badge of honor proudly worn. The wounds he suffered protecting those who enjoyed his road fazed him not. The pinches, pulls, pokes, and slaps of a toddler fazed him not. Lester took his lumps. He knew his purpose. Once we were safely back to our front yard, Lester would finally sit, or perhaps lie down, to enjoy a prolonged rub about the neck or a belly scratch for thanks. He would return to his home only once the exchange of friendship was complete. Lester was a trusted companion and a welcome alpha male. If it weren't for Lester, baseball bat or not, I never would have felt comfortable having my family out enjoying their leisure along the road in my absence.

King, Augusta, Charles, the balance of your families, and good ole Lester, thank you all. We appreciate and miss each of you. It was an honor living on your road.

CHAPTER 11

COLLAPSING CARDS AND RETURNING HOOSIERS

Lessons on Family, True Friends, Responsibility,
Faith, Fight, and Grandpa

OVER THE COURSE OF ALMOST TEN YEARS AS A TEST DRIVER WITH Michelin, I learned, enjoyed, and experienced many great things. I developed a few deep friendships and grew reasonably close to many other fine people. Sure, there were some downsides, as there are with any job, but they did little to tarnish the whole. Brian and I rose to the top of our craft and the top of our group. Guys like us, with the skill sets we possessed, were needed less and less as Michelin and its culture evolved into the early 2000s.

The challenge of the role just wasn't there anymore, and the strictest requirements of driving excellence relaxed. We felt the need to adjust our trajectories. For the last few months of 2003 and the first half of 2004, Brian and I worked long and hard to frame our future years as independent-contract drivers, offering back to Michelin many of the same test services we had provided as employees. By mid-June 2004, the stage was set, the contracts were signed, and the announcements were made much to the surprise and chagrin of our fellow drivers, who knew nothing of our developments. Brian and I were leaving Michelin but would remain familiar faces at the track, or so we thought.

I returned home that Monday morning, June 28, 2004, at something like 9:00 AM to Tekoa's surprised and concerned reception. I'm sure, in my countenance, she imagined that she was looking at a ghost. I wasn't supposed to be in our driveway on a Monday morning at 9:00 AM. I was supposed to be at the track, working. I was in our driveway, however, the proudest of men now home, clenching a contract that likely wasn't worth the paper on which it was printed and probably without my corporate position to which I could revert. A few days later, both suspicions were confirmed. No contract would be honored without a legal battle, and I was no longer welcome in my previous position. Our house of cards had fallen.

I was an unemployed test driver with a wonderful wife, a twenty-two-month-old son, a beautiful eleven-acre property, a new home, a mortgage with a balance of $150,000, and the closest blood relative some six hundred fifty miles away. *Humbling*, *humiliating*, *deflating*, and *infuriating* are all pitifully inadequate words to describe the torrent of emotions raging within me, Tekoa's husband, Sawyer's father, Paul and Pam's son, whose responsibility it was to love, to lead, and to provide for his family.

The details of this collapse, the lessons learned, and the long-term effects on multiple lives are story enough of their own—another book, another time. Some seventeen years later, it remains difficult at times for me to unlock my jaw and crack open the grip I hold on bitter feelings from that experience. I wouldn't wish something like that on anyone. From the ashes, however, emerged powerful examples of friendship as well as opportunities for mentorship I might otherwise have missed, or to which I might have otherwise been blind. Our good Lord continues to challenge me through this experience. He reminds me that we are to forgive those who trespass against us in the same way we expect to be forgiven of our own transgressions against Him and others. We are to find and radiate light and hope, no matter the depths of darkness.

Tekoa loved me through it all. She assured me that it would all be okay, that we would find our way, that we still had each other, and that all the rest could be salvaged. Brian, though he could easily have assigned blame for the collapse entirely to me, could easily have abandoned me and continued on with Michelin, chose not to. He chose instead to continue as the supportive friend he had always been, leaving Michelin on his own terms, if for no other reason than pure principle. What had happened wasn't right. He knew it wasn't right, and he chose to leave.

Brian and I explored options. We worked through scenarios. We shared deep grief that knows before knowing that our lives would change immensely and immediately. Our worlds would diverge. Our friendship would be taxed by distance, but it would not be diminished. We were tight. We would miss each other and the daily benefit of our friendship, but neither we nor our bond would be broken.

In life, most of us probably hope for at least as many true friends as could be counted on one hand. Brian takes one of those positions for me. No truer friend can be found. Thanks, man. You have helped make me a better driver, a better friend, a better man. I'm sorry things went the way they did and that you and your family had to endure so much. Someday, somehow, perhaps we will understand why all this happened the way that it did, perhaps not. Regardless, I can't thank you enough for being such a good friend.

Being only days before the Fourth of July, our young family traveled back to Indiana for the holiday with the heaviest of hearts. I arranged a family meeting with my siblings and my parents to explain the difficult situation I'm sure all sensed in my voice and manner. I explained just enough of the details for high-level understanding but withheld most others in a sorry attempt to conceal my bitterness. I explained that we planned to sell our new homestead in South Carolina and return to Indiana to be close to family. I planned to secure a regular job, and our family would settle into a new normal. No one judged, blamed, or prodded for additional information.

They just loved and supported wherever they could. That's what family does.

I dusted, updated, and distributed my résumé for conventional engineering work and crafted a new one pursuant to interests I had in construction. We went about finding the right house and piece of property to call home. Dad, with his past experience and up-to-date license as a real-estate broker, was invaluable in our property search. With Dad's help and financing, we purchased a simple, modern country place, well situated just outside of town but close enough to everything that town has to offer. Dad's half of the real-estate commission went directly to our loan with him. He allowed no debate.

With eleven goats and two dogs in South Carolina, space and accommodations were needed for at least some of these critters to move to Indiana. Even before we closed on our Indiana property, we started the fencing process. Dad and I collected materials on-site, much to the displeasure of the sellers, even though they had agreed to such preparations. My siblings and I were shaking the bushes for local engineering opportunities, including at Caterpillar, where Shawn was a well-respected technician. By the end of the Fourth of July holiday, the proverbial skies turned a lighter shade of gray. Still, we returned to South Carolina with much to do in preparation for the unplanned uproot.

We had our South Carolina house and property to prepare and sell. We had to plan the move and pack our things. We had to shut off services and say goodbye to friends. Many were still clueless that any change had taken place. Those were simpler, more genuine days before Facebook, Twitter, Instagram, and all the rest. In the midst of it all, there was still one significant bit of driving business I had to complete. It was Supercar Challenge time again. As before, in 2002, Brian and I were hired by Hennessey Performance and Lingenfelter Performance Engineering, respectively, to put their companies on the podium. I was once again a sugar cookie, however. The Michelin debacle had sent me far into the surf and deep into the proverbial sand. I was flailing about and brushing off, desperately trying to find a way to move forward.

For this event, we drove both directions with Brian's Dad, Larry. Larry, like many others, is a true friend with nothing but support to offer. It is small wonder that Brian is the man he is with parents like Larry and Beverly. Larry, of course, knew well of my situation, having heard the details from Brian. Larry and I, however, had not yet run across each other since the cards had fallen.

When I arrived at Brian's house and was in the process of parking my car, moving my things to our traveling vehicle, saying hellos and how-are-yous to Larry, and trying to appear fully recovered and ready for our road trip, Larry stopped me in my tracks with pain in his own eyes. He embraced me as a man embraces a friend at a funeral who's lost a brother. He didn't say anything I can recall. By his embrace, he just took what he could of my pain unto himself. Larry was a staunch supporter, almost like another Southern father. Larry knew what Brian was going through for me. Larry felt what I was going through, and he was pulling and praying for me and my family. That morning in Brian's driveway meant as much to me as all of our weekends of adventure at tracks and airports throughout the country over our racing years. I really appreciated your support, Larry. I may never have told you directly in so many words, but I surely did. Thank you.

As one might imagine, our trip to Michigan was abnormally somber but not without hope and resolve. We had jobs to do and great people from great companies to represent. For the Lingenfelter team and me, however, a repeat victory was not to be. We were competing in two classes. In the sedan class, we fielded a naturally aspirated, but surprisingly potent, Cadillac CTS-V. In the open class, it was another twin-turbo 427 Corvette. John Lingenfelter had passed away the previous Christmas, following his tragic crash. His presence was sorely missed, but his high-caliber team did well to carry on in his absence.

My driving was sharp but was not as sharp as it needed to be that day. I lacked my edge, my moxie. From the Cadillac, I extracted the vast majority of performance the car had to offer. It was enough to bring home a tie for third place. With the Corvette, the elements of a victory were coming together but neither in big enough chunks nor fast enough. I struggled to optimize the clutch at launch in this particular car, and I hadn't put together a particularly noteworthy lap in my first four attempts. When time came for my fifth and final run, the car died unexpectedly in the staging area, requiring a boost to start again. Once restarted, the car had a number of troubling warning indicators on the dash, one being the ABS light, which refused to go out. There was no time to diagnose or fix the problem, and we didn't know if the issue was genuine or perhaps simply a leftover from the required jump start. It was our turn to stage and launch. We were not allowed to dillydally on the line.

I stayed away from the ABS threshold for the road course and had a decent run going, but I had no idea if I would or would not have ABS going into the all-important 150–0 mph braking zone. Either having ABS or not having ABS would have been okay, but not knowing was a real problem. I did not end up having the benefit of ABS, and, with that brief stretch of tire lockup that proved it, victory slipped beyond our reach, literally. We trailed first place by a slim margin.

Brian and the Hennessey Viper performed well all day, staying just in front of any numbers I could achieve with the Corvette. The race was won that day by the better driver in the better car. It was a fitting conclusion, but it certainly was not the way I wanted it to go for the Lingenfelter team. Congratulations, Brian and Hennessey Performance! You guys won that one fair and square. Well done!

Back to South Carolina and our unwelcome move. It would be nice to mention by name each of the good folks in South Carolina who offered kind words and lent their support in the middle of the mess. There are many colleagues, friends, and neighbors—good folks we really appreciate and miss. Though he is little more than five feet and a few inches tall, for me, Charles stands quietly and figuratively tall among them.

It was a beautiful late-summer Saturday. The Penske truck was backed up to our house, and we were loading with purpose. Shawn and Dad had traveled down with me to load and haul the bulk of our things back to Indiana. We had much to do and little time in which to get it done. Charles stopped over to check on us and see if he could be of some help. Beautiful though it was in terms of weather, this was a dark and desolate day for me. I was angry and in a deep, resentful funk. I didn't want to move, and I didn't want outside help. My family and I were doing just fine. We were getting it done, and I surely didn't want to engage my reverent, kindly neighbor in conversation about the move.

I wanted to be test-driving and racing as always. I wanted to be watching our son playing in the yard and taking walks down Dixon Road with my wife. I wanted to be progressing on the shop and studio apartment I was building. I wanted to be enjoying the life young married couples were supposed to enjoy, not packing our belongings for an unwanted move. Tekoa and I had dreamed and worked extremely hard to develop our family and our property to that point. Why would we want to move? I was very angry. Thankfully, I kept all of that bottled up at the time and politely, but dismissively, thanked Charles for his offer.

Charles reflected for a short time, then silently started loading things.

Though I didn't want his help in that moment, I wasn't about to ask Charles to leave us alone with our sorry task. I had far too much respect for him, and I'm certain God directed me to just chill out and let Charles be Charles. Charles was very helpful, and his help was indeed appreciated. His work ethic and quality were both exceptional, and his pace was more in line with a man half his actual age. As the last few majors were loaded, and it became obvious that there were more hands on deck than the remaining space in the truck could support, Charles said a few words of support before departing and closed by asking about our plans for the evening and the next day.

Knowing that our vehicles were packed, along with most of our food and drink, Charles invited us to dinner. We politely declined, suggesting that we would unhook one of the trailers and squeeze into some vehicle for a trip in town. We needed to do so anyway to attend church that evening or the following morning before heading north. Charles all but insisted that we use his car for both purposes since ours were packed and that we each take a beverage to enjoy later in the evening. Ashamed of my dismal attitude and spirit, I hung my head with a subtle shake and yielded to Charles's kindness. We did borrow his car for dinner and church, and we did enjoy those beverages later.

In his own way, Charles, the Good Samaritan, dressed my wounds, loaded me on his animal, and paid the innkeeper for my stay. Charles exemplifies kindness and service. I regret not having befriended him more completely and drawn more deeply from his wisdom while in South Carolina. Thank you, Charles. I miss you, my friend.

My disastrous departure from Michelin exposed me to the bowels of humanity, and the years since our move back to Indiana in the fall of 2004 have not always been easy. But, the difficult experiences and the times of struggle have carried out some of God's purposes within me. They have made me a better son, a better father, a better husband, a better man, and a better leader of our family with greater character and deeper faith in God. I would not trade these experiences and difficult years. They have been my forge.

SIDEBAR 6:

RESPONSIBILITY, FAITH, AND FIGHT

What better place than here for another important sidebar, this one on responsibility, faith, and struggle against evil and vice. Here's my summary:

> You are responsible for your actions. God exists, as do moral and natural absolutes. There is right and wrong. You will experience some of each. Right brings peace. Wrong causes pain. When you choose to do right, relish the peace and strive to do more. When you choose to do wrong, own the pain, learn the lesson, and resolve to do better next time. Seek guidance. You don't know it all. The Bible and folks who live Christ's teachings with fruit on the tree are great places to start.

I am well credentialed to assert that you and I will mess up in life. Since there are absolutes, and relativism is a useless excuse for failure, we must accept our shortcomings and mistakes. We learn from them but should never surrender the fight to improve. We are fallen people living in a fallen world. Sometimes our mess-ups are self-induced, and our responsibility is undeniable. Other times we might get caught up in something that seems out of our control, something for which it may seem we shouldn't be held accountable. It doesn't matter. Get over it. The sooner we accept that life is not fair, that we are not owed or entitled to anything merely by our existence, the sooner we will make meaningful progress. We must take responsibility, full responsibility, for our lives, the actions we take, and the results we produce.

> You are your own result.

God who? Faith what? In current American culture, little is considered sacred, honored, or cherished. Truth is left open to interpretation relative to its impact on me and my "rights." Not even life itself is respected in our times. Forcibly harvested human body parts, large and small, are available for purchase. The rights of the preborn and the captives and destitute from whom they are harvested—who cares about those? Adult males can walk into a Target bathroom alongside preschool girls if they claim to feel feminine. The rights and feelings of preschool girls—who cares about those? Why bother keeping foul language and nudity out of public broadcasting? Kids hear that stuff and see most of it in school anyway. Everybody's doing it, even some teachers. What are morals anyway? Everything is relative, right? All the answers you'll ever need can be constructed with science—just ask most academics. Get Bibles and prayer out of schools and public assemblies. While we are at it, why not just go ahead and extract "under God" from our national anthem and "In God We Trust" from our currency. We're so smart; we have this all figured out and don't need Him anymore.

A sad number of people—or perhaps that should be a number of sad people—have respect neither for this great country they call home nor for their neighbors with whom they share it. Our currency is tanking along with our financial intelligence. The value of our dollar is dropping like a rock while the Fed prints more, and Americans continue living on money they don't have. If it feels good, tastes good, looks good, impresses people, contributes to our plush convenience, and doesn't seem to hurt anyone directly, why wouldn't it be okay? I'm the only one who really matters. It's all about me and what I want, right? Wrong.

Such thinking is flawed, foolish, shortsighted, and self-defeating. There is a God, and it isn't your or I. There are natural laws and foundational guideposts for life with which we must not tamper. There are moral absolutes for which we must stand firm. Virtue, character, honor, courage, and, yes, life and faith matter immensely. My granddad, my dad, the fine men and women referenced in this book, and many other inspiring characters agree with me. You may not agree with me, and that's okay. That indeed is one of your rights in this great country, to disagree with or ignore what I know to be true. You are also welcome to disagree with or ignore the truth of gravity. Just don't reach out for my hand when you decide to test your version of truth by jumping off a bridge. See how valuable your truth is then.

Dad was born and raised Catholic. His childhood was disciplined and strict with regard to faith. Dad continued in this way. He did his best to raise my siblings and me with this biblical system of beliefs, anchored to the Ten Commandments, the Beatitudes, and life examples from Jesus Christ. We almost never missed worship. On rare occasions, we might miss church, such as when we were traveling with no church in the area. We almost never missed worship, however. I distinctly remember this situation on a number of family vacations. Traveling down the road in the motor home, having missed any local church service, the whole family would gather at the front of the coach, praying the rosary, each of us with his own contribution.

Cussing and carrying on, disrespecting others, lying, stealing, cheating, having sex outside of marriage, doing drugs, using alcohol to excess—each of these and many more were things you just didn't do. Neither spiritual life nor secular life would go well for you if you played with such matches. Eventually, you would get burned, and you would do harm to yourself, to your loved ones, and to your family in the process. We did not have long, in-depth conversations about any of this. Rather, we knew what was expected because we saw it lived out each day at home and in our community. Snares and pitfalls such as those above, which others in our society flirted with or openly courted, were to be avoided at all costs. In society at large, and occasionally closer to home, we would see the destructive effects of ignorance or indifference in these areas.

To be sure, though, life is tough—much more easily professed well than lived well. Friends, circumstances, and courted temptations can be incredibly difficult to resist. Once fallen, one finds it more difficult to rise again and retain his footing on better ground. Dad understands this. I recall one particular time in my life, unrelated to the Michelin debacle or any other sugar-cookie event, where I was struggling hard against one or another temptation or challenge to my biblical commitment. I had been fighting hard for some time, and I was exhausted. I needed some encouragement. I called home and asked to talk with Dad. Mom handed him the phone, and he answered with words and a tone that made me think he had been expecting my call. Shocker!

I explained my plight, fighting back strong emotions commensurate with the situation and my struggle against it. I explained my perception that his generation and Grandpa's generation and other generations prior must have been stronger, more disciplined, more pure, more resolute, perhaps—something more, something stronger. I believed I was failing in my battle, and I surmised that previous generations had held fast with nary a rearward step. I needed his secret. I needed an explanation of how this could be so in order to continue fighting my fight with vigor. I was near the end of my rope.

His response, while well tailored to my situation at that time, contains timeless insights and encouragement useful to anyone aspiring to be his best self, regardless of the season or the plight: "Son, my dad's generation wasn't perfect, my generation wasn't perfect, and I wasn't perfect, either. God doesn't expect perfection. He looks for faith, and He expects persistence. He expects you to fight the good fight and never give up. Reconciliation is there if, or when, you stumble. *But*, you never accept defeat, and you never stay down. I love you, Son."

There is a lot to unpack in those few sentences. Dad didn't speak to any particular vice or temptation. He didn't throw anyone under the bus, and he didn't claim personal perfection for himself. He also didn't hand me a pass. Rather, Dad acknowledged reality and the difficulty of the crosses we sometimes bear. He concluded with a fortified reminder of God's expectation, God's love and mercy, and his own clear instruction to fight on tirelessly with the assurance of his support and love. I hope, when my day comes, I can be as clear and helpful to our kids.

No one is perfect, but never cease trying
to be the best that you can be.

CLEM AND HELEN GESWEIN, 1931

I would like to close this sidebar and wrap this chapter up by shining additional light on the life of my grandfather. His example, too, inspires me. These reflections bring conclusion in a way I believe to be both thought-provoking and complete. They invite each of us to consider God's mysterious plans and our roles within those plans. I still ponder how and why I was privileged to be bedside at the moment this good Hoosier returned home.

In September 2005, Dad's dad, my grandpa Geswein, died at the age of ninety-five. Though I haven't mentioned much about Grandpa to this point, he certainly was a positive influence for me and a strong role model for many. The courage, character, and faith he carried with him in this earthly life and into the next left an impression I will not forget. I was at his bedside, the only person at his bedside, when he died. His return home to be with the Lord is a story of its own. Before getting there, I need to share a few earlier elements of Grandpa's life. Sharing these extra details will help frame his influence and heavenly return.

Grandpa Geswein was born in 1910 in Lanesville, Indiana, the son of hardworking farm parents. Recently married, Grandpa and his wife, Helen, pulled up their proverbial roots in search of a better life and more fertile soil, literally, in northwestern Indiana. They settled in the countryside not far from Dunnington. Grandpa and Grandma had little at the time of their settling in this community. Grandpa worked for several local farmers, eventually purchasing his first piece of farm ground. That first piece of ground eventually became just one piece of the vast, well-respected Circle Drive Farms, which he and Grandma developed. Together they conceived and raised seven boys and one girl. JoAnn, their only daughter, was killed along with her husband in a tragic plane crash upon return from their honeymoon. Each of the seven sons went on to marry, then conceive and raise seventeen children total in their own families. The Geswein presence in our community grew quickly.

I remember Grandpa as a simple, devout Catholic man, somewhat small in physical stature, quiet and reserved, always working on something, and never complaining about anything. In many ways, he was similar to my friend Charles in South Carolina. Grandpa wasn't an obviously affectionate man in his words or public displays, but he was undoubtedly a devoted family man whose family was certain of his love. When necessary, Grandpa expressed love indirectly through discipline. Grandpa understood Proverbs 13:24 (mentioned in the second sidebar on parenting and discipline). Grandpa applied discipline swiftly and fairly.

He loved his children enough to train them properly, and he provided correction when needed. Dad shares his early reflections with me about Grandpa both respectfully and thankfully. Dad loved and respected his father.

Grandpa seemed always to have his rosary. He never missed church or fell short on obligations. I picture him still, scouring the fields for rocks with his 1948 Ford 8N tractor. He seldom wore jeans, more often olive drab pants or coveralls. Grandpa never owned a pickup truck. While it's perhaps a bit odd for a farmer not to own a pickup, Grandpa always preferred to drive a nice car that was clean and tidy. On occasional Sunday afternoons, he enjoyed relaxing with a cigar. As a kid, I once bought him a fancy cigar while on vacation. You could do that in the seventies and eighties if a parent was with you. I don't think he ever smoked that fancy cigar, but he was clearly tickled to receive it.

Grandpa liked baseball, the Chicago Cubs being his favorite team. I was honored that he would occasionally come watch me play Little League ball. Perhaps I was the only grandchild who was at the right age at the right time for him to be able to attend. Maybe we had a unique attachment for some other reason. Perhaps it was the cigar. Regardless of the reason, he came to watch me play from time to time, and I appreciated his being there.

My brother and I served as altar boys regularly at church, and I often read on Sunday mornings. I started reading at church as a very young boy who needed a box to stand at the lectern. Hearing Grandpa's few words of affirmation after church always pumped me up with a little extra pride. His words encouraged me to always do my best. Whether I was working the fields, catching behind the plate, or reading God's Word, I worked hard to make Grandpa proud.

Grandpa and Grandma watched with great pride as their children developed, found their places in life, and grew their careers and their families. Several of my uncles, Dad's brothers, continued farming and built Circle Drive Farms into something that Grandpa had only dreamed of. He watched with amazement at and appreciation of the rate and volume at which corn and soybeans streamed into the farm's granaries. It was something quite different from when he and Grandma had first established the farm with so much labor and so much love many years earlier.

Grandpa had one glass eye, odd bumps on his forearms that became more pronounced with time, and various other health challenges. You wouldn't know any of this to talk with him.

Grandpa never complained. He never allowed poor attitude or sluggish behavior to accelerate the effects of aging.

Somewhere around age seventy-five, being less involved physically in farming, Grandpa started an exercise routine that included lots of walking, push-ups, climbing his basement stairs two at a time, and resistance training using elastic bands. Grandpa continued this routine almost until his death in 2005. On one particular occasion, at a family gathering in 1999, his great-grandson Aaron, who was perhaps eleven at the time, could not fathom that his great-grandfather could do ten push-ups. Aaron could barely do ten himself. Aaron watched with wide-eyed amazement as Great-Grandpa finished his tenth push-up at nearly ninety years old with better form than Aaron himself could muster.

I remember a story from the mid-1980s where foul language repeatedly reached his table from a similarly aged man at a local restaurant not far from where he and Grandma were sitting. Grandpa asked the man to clean up his language or step outside. That sort of language was welcome neither in a family establishment nor in the presence of Helen. Grandpa was not afraid to stand for what was right. Over the years, on many occasions, I have witnessed similar situations where my dad shielded our family from such language and negative influences. I, too, have had to take this stand for my family. As has been correctly stated and repeated over many years, you've got to stand for something, or you'll fall for anything. Grandpa stood firmly upon his beliefs.

In the waning days of August 2005, at the ripe old age of ninety-five, Grandpa was situated in a comfortable bed at home where his favorite chair had been positioned for many years. His latest ailment was understood to be the tip of the proverbial iceberg of cancer that was ravaging his body. He had fought hard against cancer in other forms and other places previously, but this cancer was widespread and aggressive. He was ready to rejoin Helen. She had returned home some nine years prior. Grandpa knew down to the day how long she had been away from him. He missed her, and he was ready to be with her again eternally. The wonderful folks from hospice were there to tend to his needs and keep him comfortable. They predicted he would last six to eight days.

Grandpa was ready for death and eternal
reward. He was not the least bit scared.

True to form, he never complained about anything and didn't need anything. He just lay there imagining the reunion with his wife and three children who had preceded him in death.

We visited Grandpa on a number of occasions that week. We noticed his slow decline with each visit but treasured the opportunities to share a few words and memories with him. Lord only knows how many times Grandpa prayed the rosary in those final days. The string of beads was always in his hands. Leaving one of those early visits, I decided that Grandpa might enjoy listening to Gregorian chants as his hours passed. On the next visit, I placed a small CD player at the foot of the bed near his TV and asked the staff to continue playing the CD on "Repeat" as long as Grandpa was enjoying it. It was a long CD, *Chant* (performed by the Benedictine Monks of Santo Domingo de Silos), nineteen songs that played for nearly one hour before repeating.

The afternoon of Friday, September 2, 2005, developed with distinct, divinely delivered urgings. I was relieved to be heading home from work as I would be on any Friday afternoon following a long week. More importantly, I felt certain that I needed to load up my family promptly and proceed with some haste to see Grandpa. I believe it was Grandpa's seventh day of hospice care. I called Tekoa so that she and Sawyer could be ready to load and leave without delay. We were off again to Grandpa's farm. We wasted no time in transit. Something told me to hustle.

When we arrived at the farm, it was suppertime, and all of Grandpa's regular visitors had left to eat with their families. The hospice nurse, a friend of our family, motioned me in to Grandpa's bedside and quietly left the room that I might have some private time with him. Tekoa and Sawyer stayed outside. Grandpa looked ready but not nearly at the threshold between life and death. The monks were chanting softly, and Grandpa's eyes and mouth were open. His breathing was extended but regular. I sat beside him, not knowing what to say or if he could even hear me. I recall thanking him for being a good grandfather, for raising a good man to be my dad, and for being a good example for me to emulate. I thanked him for coming to watch me play baseball. In the brief moments it took for me to say these things, Grandpa's eyes slowly transitioned closed, and his breathing extended. The monks chanted on.

I suspected Grandpa might be drifting back to sleep. His breathing became very extended. Finally, he drew a deep, choppy breath that inflated his entire torso. As he exhaled slowly and completely, the monks concluded their final chant as if on divine cue. Grandpa went home at that moment, his eyes closed, his rosary beads comfortably in hand, and chanting monks now respectfully silent. His CD did not repeat this time. My time with him in this final visit was five minutes max, but I was there. It was an amazing, powerful experience put in motion long ago and made manifest before my eyes at just the right time. Thank you, Grandpa, for much and for allowing me to experience your triumphant homecoming. It was unforgettable, and it contributed immensely to my own faith journey.

CHAPTER 12

LOVE, LOSS, AND THE CONSTANT OF CHANGE

Lessons on New Life, Short Life, and Working
through Life's Many Challenges

STERLING AND I, 2008

Life brought many changes between 2006 and 2010, starting with the arrival of two more great kids. Tekoa and I had our precious daughter, Sterling, in 2006. Sterling arrived in a flash and has been an absolute blessing and a joy ever since. Tekoa's water broke at 2:00 AM sharp on that early May morning. Sterling greeted the world less than one hour later, at 2:50 AM. After a fifteen-minute ride to the hospital, a bypass of the whole check-in process, and a wheelchair race to the delivery room, Tekoa wasn't even given the option of an epidural. There was no time. She was "a solid nine" according to our nurse and family friend, Onalee, who happened to be on duty that morning. With one phone call en route, Onalee cleared obstructions and made hasty preparations as we traveled. A gown was quickly draped over Tekoa's shoulders to replace her normal clothing, and she was placed directly into delivery position without so much as the fitting of a hospital wristband.

Sterling's beautiful blue eyes and flowing black hair—just as vibrant then as they are today—were among the first things we saw. Now fifteen years old, Sterling remains a pure joy. She is a talented dancer with external beauty and grace that draw and fix the gaze. More important than her talent and appearance, Sterling is also abundantly kind, honest, clean, diligent, hardworking, intelligent, and courageous. She has a pure heart and is a true joy to be around. Certainly, I am biased, but trust me, this young lady is an absolute treasure with the brightest of futures.

SIEGER AND I, 2010

Less than two years later, in early January 2008, our athletic second son, Sieger, welcomed the New Year. Sieger arrived less than one week before I started a new engineering job with Caterpillar, thanks in part to Shawn's connections and solid reputation. Sieger's delivery went about as smoothly and easily as the process can go. Once again, Tekoa had no epidural. All-natural worked just great, again.

Mr. Sieger was born with a bat or a ball in his hand—figuratively, of course, but sometimes I wonder. Sieger was dribbling a basketball well and shooting hoops on a little plastic goal with surprising accuracy at only seventeen months. Baseball, his sport of choice, has been part of our lives since he was only five. Today, at age thirteen, he plays travel ball as part of the development program for our local high school. Every element of his game is superior to what mine was at his age. Catcher, third base, shortstop, first, outfield, and pitcher—he plays them all. Though he isn't supposed to do much of it yet, he can throw breaking pitches with enough movement that I have to pay close attention to keep from taking one in the face. At an honest 70 mph, his fastest pitches and longest throws are very close to the point where he can outthrow dear old

Dad. More importantly, beyond the athletics, of which he is very proud, Sieger is just a great kid. He has a kind heart, is sensitive to the pain of others, works hard in areas of importance to him, is very creative, and has a great sense of humor and adventure.

I've already spoken some of Sawyer and there is certainly more to come as his inclusion in these reflections unfolds. Undeniably and without reservation, my wife and I are extremely proud. We feel eternally blessed to have these three great kids.

Mom got to enjoy each of our kids, but only for a short time. She died too early in 2010 from cancer. Around the same time, our family started noticing some health concerns with Dad. Our young family and our extended family needed stability. We needed each other. It is one of the reasons I'm thankful that God's plan, painful though much of it has been, brought us back to Indiana when it did. I am reminded again of the prophetic words from Jeremiah: "For I know well the plans I have in mind for you, says the Lord, plans for your welfare, not for woe!"

PAMELA GESWEIN, CIRCA 1960

Through much of 2012, Dad's health and mobility was reasonable, but storm clouds were gathering. Dad and I worked a lot together between 2004 and 2012, mostly improving my new home and maintaining his. There was always something to be done. Those proved to be some of the last good years for the proverbial heavy lifting. All of the concrete pouring and finishing that Dad and I had done together in earlier years made us a better team. We poured and finished more than a hundred yards of concrete, which became my shop floor and driveway. We cut wood, replaced roofs, transplanted trees, seeded grass, ripped out walls, built fences and shelters, built a beautiful masonry hearth, and installed a wood-burning stove, among many other things. Unlike the false start we had experienced with the home and improvements in South Carolina, all of this work near family in Indiana brought with it a welcome sense of permanence and peace.

Two of Dad's older brothers had died in earlier years, each suffering the effects of Parkinson's disease at the time of his death. We hadn't seen or suspected Parkinson's plaguing Dad until maybe 2009. At that time, Mom was not in good health. Our attention was on her, not on Dad. By early April 2010, our days with Mom were very limited in number. Cancer made its way into her bones. On the morning of April 29, 2010, Pam Geswein went home. Dad lost his wife and friend of more than forty-five years. We all grieved Mom's passing, none more than Dad.

Mom and Dad had worked hard and sacrificed much throughout their younger years in order to comfortably enjoy each other and the fruits of their labors during retirement. Mom's rapidly developing cancer and death at the age of only sixty-seven cut those retirement years quite short. Hindsight is always twenty-twenty, of course. More than once I've heard Dad say with some sadness, regret perhaps,

"I should have spoiled your mother more."

Dad's lesson here is poignant. Dad did love and spoil Mom, but knowing what he knows now, he would have gone even further while he had the opportunity. Plan and save, to be sure, but love others and live each day with some fun and flair in the moment. There may not be so many tomorrows. Today, Dad sends me off from most calls and visits by saying, "Love your family." You bet, Dad.

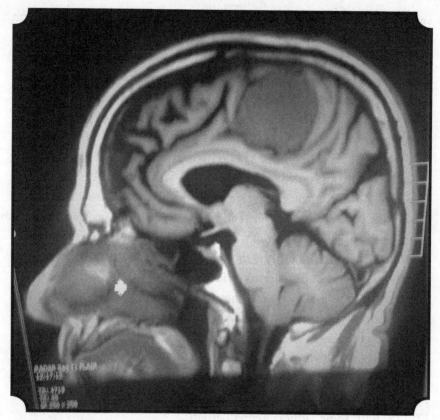

DAD'S X-RAY AND OBVIOUS BRAIN TUMOR, 2012

In the years since Mom's passing, Dad's Parkinson's disease has progressed, thankfully to a lesser degree and at a slower rate than anticipated. Dad had knee surgery twice on his left knee. He lost most of the functionality of his right leg from the prolonged pressure of a large benign tumor on the left side of his brain. For too long, doctors and family mistakenly blamed Parkinson's for his altered gait and uncooperative leg. Instead, the source of the problem was pressure building in the brain from the undetected tumor. His tumor, the size of an apricot, was successfully removed in late 2012. Mobility lost never returned. The lost mobility, while lamentable, does not stop him.

Earlier in 2012, my family and I purchased the forty-six-acre farm adjacent to Dad's house, the house I grew up in. We purchased this farm from cherished family friends the Bracketts, who had owned and loved the property as a recreation farm for more than twenty years, starting about the time I went off to college. Our families became close over those years, and we remain so still today. The Bracketts are very interesting folks with fascinating stories and valuable life lessons of their own. Andrea Brackett, in fact, with her master's degree in journalism, was kind enough to write this book's foreword as well as to edit and improve the manuscript. I am extremely grateful. Thank you, Andrea!

Since about 1993, Dad had tended the Brackett's farm in their absence, and our families enjoyed time together when everyone was in town. As a child, I rode dirt bikes, fed cattle, put up hay, shot crib rats, constructed tree houses, and acted on my brother's bidding to smoke a few cigars on this farm. Dad, too, has a long history with the farm. In the 1960s, that forty-six acres was heavily wooded. In 1965, with Mom's support, a couple of chainsaws, some axes, an old Army tent for storage, and some well-worn machinery, Dad cleared this much of this land for its owner at the time in exchange for the opportunity to buy sixteen acres to the west. Over the years, Dad went on to apply his keen eye and skills as a surveyor and equipment operator to construct a two-acre pond on the farm, as well as a pond of almost three acres on his own sixteen-acre parcel.

Despite his mobility challenges and slower pace, if there is a job to be done, Dad is still more than eager to help. To this day, there remains a section of broken shovel handle about twenty-five inches long beside the seat in the skid-steer loader at our farm. This old handle serves as a substitute for Dad's uncooperative right leg and foot. Like much equipment, particularly older equipment, this skid-steer requires both hands and both feet to operate efficiently. Each of one's four appendages controls a different function of the machine. With almost no dexterity in his right foot, Dad compensates by grabbing the old shovel handle and pushing the foot pedal, or "foot feet," as Dad calls it, to tilt the bucket. It is difficult to get Dad in and out of the machine these days, but I leave the old shovel handle by the seat just in case he feels like contorting himself and logging some hours at the helm.

DAD MANAGING A CONTROLLED BURN AT OUR FARM, 2015

One of the things Dad enjoys as much as any other is mowing grass with our John Deere 1445 commercial mower. It is a mean mowing machine, by far Dad's favorite. Nearly six of the forty-six acres at our farm is covered with grass that requires finish mowing. Starting in late April or early May, it has to be mowed every week. Some years, mowing at this rate is required until nearly October. In recent years, Dad and Sawyer have frequently been a dynamic duo for the job. Until just last year, Dad has been a fixture on the 1445. It takes a little time and a little work to get Dad from the car to the seat of the mower and back again. If he is feeling up to it, the effort is more than worth it. Running equipment turns Dad's clock back many years. Five years or so ago, I considered selling this mower to upgrade to a newer model with conventional ZTR controls. I'm glad I didn't go through with it. It is worth a few extra dollars for maintenance and a little less gloss in the finish. Seeing Dad enjoy fresh air and liberation on his favorite John Deere is priceless.

In 2014, a new chapter in Dad's life opened for a time by way of my brother, Shawn. Shawn began his career at Caterpillar in 1993. After just over twenty years, he was ready to exchange corporate work for entrepreneurship in the form of his own business hauling and operating heavy equipment. With Dad's help, he established a base of operations and procured a number of newer pieces of CAT equipment. These modern machines were controlled entirely by hand. Dexterity with one's feet, or lack thereof, mattered not. This enabled Dad to stay active and contribute physically to Shawn's developing business, which he did with some regularity through 2019. Dad ran excavators big and small, backhoes, track loaders, and bulldozers, to name but a few. Together, Shawn and Dad razed houses, cleared tree lines, built ponds, and dug basements. They even dismantled an old factory with storage silos considerably taller than the biggest of his excavators.

After two years of helping Shawn, the growing challenge of getting in and out of the equipment made it more difficult for Dad to participate. In late 2016, with the help of some fantastic mobility-enhancing equipment from Life Essentials in Wolcott, Indiana, Dad was mobilized and empowered to continue equipment operation yet a few more years.

DAD FINISH-GRADING WITH A RAKE FROM HIS TRACKCHAIR, 2017

In the time it has taken me to write this book, it has become increasingly difficult for Dad to get around and do much of the manual labor he enjoys. Though he is rarely on a mower or in a piece of heavy equipment today, Dad is not finished working. He is always ready, at least in spirit, to help, and there are certainly still good days when Dad can get out and help physically. "Let me know if I can help" is something I've heard Dad say so often it just comes out like muscle memory from his mouth and vocals. Whenever Dad's day comes, these might be his final words. It would be fitting, really. Perhaps a perfect way to close this particular chapter is by way of a fitting quote most often ascribed to Gandhi:

"Love as if you'll die tomorrow.
Work as if you'll live forever."

CHAPTER 13

MOVING ON

Reflections and Lessons on Mentorship, Toxins, and True Freedom

IN 2016, I LEFT THE COMFORT, THE BENEFITS, THE STABILITY, AND THE pay of my engineering job at Caterpillar in search of a better fit and more joy. For at least four of the eight years I worked for Caterpillar, I was fortunate to benefit directly from the friendship and mentorship of Ron, an engineering manager at CAT. We remain friends, and Ron is a trusted mentor yet today, though I have been lax about maintaining regular communications with him. Ron contributed to my life and my tenure at Caterpillar in various ways, not the least of which was his support of my decision to leave. That's right; he supported me and my decision to leave in several ways. Two in particular are worthy of note in these reflections.

First, Ron recognized and affirmed that I must be true to myself for my own health and that of my family. He commended my work and the reputation I had built for myself at CAT. He also clarified that CAT wasn't going anywhere. He assured me that, to the extent of his control, I could always come back. Though I'm sure he doubted that I would return, he knew it was important for me to understand that CAT's safety net would most likely be there. No family provider feels comfortable shutting off a reliable stream of funds and security for his loved ones simply because he is less than satisfied with his role.

Second, and more poignantly, Ron made a statement to our children in the closing stages of my farewell lunch that I will never forget. My boss, my close coworkers and friends, my wife, and our kids were all in attendance. Ron focused his attention, and the attention of the whole table, on my kids until the group grew quiet. He looked each of our kids squarely in their young faces and said, "You have a great dad," in a way that seemed purposeful and deliberate. I've speculated several times as to why Ron said that and why he delivered the words the way that he did. I don't have an answer. Perhaps his words just came out that way without motive or design. I doubt it. I am very grateful for Ron and his kind words. I've needed to reflect on Ron's declaration on several dark days since that lunch. His mentorship and support have been great helps for me. Thank you, Ron.

For the better part of twelve months following my departure from Caterpillar, I served as the general manager of my mother-in-law's small manufacturing business. I enjoyed the work, I like the staff, and I believe I added value. Two things, however, limited progress to such an extent that it was best for me to leave.

First, there was a man involved in the business who was not a good influence on anyone. I needed to get away from him. Muffled voices around the shop referred to him as "the troll." Unfortunately, I was not given the authority to remove him. Day in and day out, this man rolled from one manufacturing area to another, grumbling, complaining, or badmouthing someone or something. There is no doubt that this man is intelligent, experienced, and often replete with legitimate points. Sadly, however, he was also laden with so much disdain for others and so little professionalism or respect that few noticed or cared about any of the good stuff he had to offer.

On one particular afternoon, this man rolled into my office around 4:30 as the crew was completing their cleanup tasks for the day. He clumsily ran his powered chair into the desk I occupied. Such was his habit. He leaned forward my direction onto his elbows and forearms as if to brace himself for the force of the hate he was about to expel. I knew what was coming. I had heard and seen it all before. As I looked into his eyes, and he began to spew verbal toxin, I checked out. Mentally, I stepped outside for a breath of fresh air, and I lost any content beyond his first sentence. How does a person get like this? Knowing I had no authority to remove him from the company, I said to myself, *That's it!* In that moment, my process of departure began. I mentally resigned. I refused to continue spending my time and investing my labors in the same sphere as someone with such a foul spirit. Life is too short to remain in the presence of such folks.

This man has redeeming qualities—somewhere. I did plenty of time, almost twelve months, trying to find, focus on, and highlight those qualities for myself and others. No more was I going to sift endlessly through obnoxious spoils to unearth that which was redeeming. Either he was leaving or I was. I had better things to do and better people to be around. You don't need to be mean, nasty, unprofessional, or unloving, but your life is a result of your choices. Sometimes you must choose better associations. That's what I had to do. As the popular motivational speaker Les Brown famously implores,

"It's necessary to get the losers out of your life!"

Besides this man's toxic influence, the second reason I had to leave was that I was swimming upstream against a cultural current I could fight only so far without creating problems in my relationship with Tekoa. Recall I was working for her mother's business. My marriage is far more important than any job. It was time for me to go.

Not so many years ago, in a career-development class at Caterpillar, the presenter made an assertion that resonated with me by its simplicity and truth. He suggested that the career paths a person is most likely to enjoy are those that resemble or relate to things enjoyed during the formative adolescent years. In those years, I was supremely happy farming, being outside working on most anything, and imbibing everything motorsports. In the many years that have followed my adolescence, certainly other interests and pleasures have been identified and added, but the simplicity and true joys of my youth have endured.

DAD AND I AT HOME, CIRCA 1974; MY BROTHER, SHAWN, AT
RIGHT WITH OUR PRESENT DAY FARM IN THE BACKGROUND

By God's plan, my buddy Brian and I had stayed in reasonable contact over the years and our friendship had remained strong. After leaving Michelin when we did in 2004, Brian continued down a motorsports path. He spent several years managing a track in South Carolina and training folks individually on the side. Later, he moved to Utah, where he became general manager of the Ford Performance Racing School (FPRS). Brian was instrumental in helping the school grow to its current size and stature as one of the biggest and best high-performance driving programs in the country. He also spearheaded the school's recent move to Charlotte, North Carolina. In 2017, Brian was looking to expand the services offered by the school. He was looking to expand services into an area much closer to

Ford's worldwide headquarters in Dearborn, Michigan. Due to my past Ford connections, my physical proximity in Indiana, my contentment behind the wheel, and our friendship, the conditions were right for my career path and Brian's to converge once again.

In the spring of 2017, I left "conventional" work, formed my own business, and set out anew behind the wheel and at the front of a classroom, providing driver training, instruction, testing, and driving-event support. My reintroduction to this work after having been mostly on hiatus for thirteen years was a bit uncomfortable but most welcome. It began when Brian called to explain that a big event was going on at his track in Utah and that he needed my help. The new Ford GT—Ford's 216 mph, half-million-dollar supercar—was being introduced to the worldwide press, and a few trusted drivers were needed to ride as right-seat passengers while the journalists drove. The expectation was that journalists would behave better by having a professional driver in the right seat. Additionally, the professional driver could prove helpful in preventing problems before they became unmanageable.

Ford GT and I, Sonoma Raceway, 2018

The behavior of most journalists turned out to be relatively benign, and their skill levels were adequate, but several needed remedial instruction for driving at that level. Riding right seat was not comfortable. Imagine being on a roller coaster capable of more than 200 mph without any rails, guides, or mechanical limits. Imagine that you are merely a passenger, no wheel or pedals of your own. You are along for the ride, trusting in the skill and judgment of someone proficient at writing about fast cars but perhaps unvetted for suitability to drive one. Further, imagine that the driver of this half-million-dollar missile is released like a hungry cheetah from a cage into an arena of gazelles. Journalists were allowed three laps on a twelve-turn, 2.2-mile, racetrack with minimal rules.

Ford's development of this car and the chance for journalists to drive it had been years in the making. The day came, and there was a palpable air of excitement and competition among the journalists who were invited to participate. Some journalists were pretty good. Some were not. Those who were not so good tested my vomit resistance much more than they tested the actual limits of this awesome car. To endure erratic driving in a Ford Focus with 130 horsepower and all-season tires is one thing. To stomach erratic driving in a Ford GT with almost 650 horsepower and grip galore, on the other hand, is something entirely different. In 2004, when I had last ridden with other drivers at speed, this sort of thing didn't bother me much. Thirteen years later, I was thankful for Dramamine.

Thanks to Brian and the confidence and friendship he has shown in opening this door for me, I am considerably happier at work. I'm gone from home more frequently, but, overall, I work fewer hours. I'm happier in every hour I spend working, and the remaining hours at home with family are far richer.

While I have a number of customers for whom I provide driving and instruction services, FPRS is my most regular customer. FPRS delivers professional, high-performance driving programs like a well-oiled machine. The instructors are top-caliber drivers and fun folks to be around. They take their craft and the quality of the customer experience very seriously. In the last three years, I've had the opportunity to ride, drive, and instruct in all of the Ford Performance products, from the Fiesta ST and F-150

Raptor to the Ford GT and Shelby GT500, in environments stretching from Utah's mountains and California's hills to Ford's Michigan Proving Ground and the famed Charlotte Motor Speedway. It has been a pleasure working with these great products and great people as I hone my craft once again. Brian, Dan, and the FPRS team, thank you.

CHAPTER 14

LIVING TOWARD LEGACY

Lessons on Marksmanship, Timeless Investments,
SPG, and Conservative Education

THE YEAR 2017 WAS A MILESTONE YEAR FOR ANOTHER GOOD REASON: DAD turned eighty years old. It was time to throw him a surprise party. We started planning the party early in the year, months before his July birthday. Such things take time and careful planning, particularly if your plans include the element of surprise. His surprise party was to happen at our farm. Since purchasing the farm in 2012, we had made many improvements, including upgrading the electrical and water service, installing hundreds of feet of drainage tile, pouring more concrete, building more fence and structures, and completely remaking the hay barn for events and family celebrations. Finally, we had built out a "cottage" on the floor level of the barn so that we could stay over in comfort any time we wished. Dad had a hand in almost all of these projects. It was only fitting that his birthday celebration take place at our farm. The date was set for Saturday, July 1, 2017.

To appreciate the climax of Dad's celebration, we need a bit of background. Dad has always been a good marksman. He is an excellent shot and had enjoyed using the same beloved shotgun for as long as I had been alive: a near-mint-condition late-sixties 20-gauge Remington 1100 semiautomatic. I have distant memories of going to a few skeet shoots with Dad when I was very young, just old enough to recall a few fragmented scenes and features.

I don't recall how Dad fared in those shoots so long ago, but I'm certain he would have been in the running for a win. When we were kids, whether it was varmints or clay pigeons, if Dad had his 1100 on the target, the subject's future and form was about to change. Some eight or nine years prior, however, his beloved shotgun had disappeared. To be more precise, it was sold—yes, sold. One of his grandsons, in a fit of adolescent foolishness, sold this cherished gun that Dad had *loaned* him for the hunting season. Apparently, this young grandson somehow came to believe that the gun had been given to him as a forever gift rather than simply on loan for seasonal use. Armed with this faulty belief, Grandson decided to sell Grandpa's gun for cash. With the cash and the help of his buddy's father, he turned around and purchased something more exciting, something like a crossbow.

Once completed and subsequently discovered, the clandestine transactions could not be undone. The unsuspecting new owner of Dad's gun would have none of it. In the following years, this purchaser passed away, leaving the gun in his estate. The gun somehow made its way to Missouri with the girlfriend of one of the purchaser's descendants. I'm sure there are additional twists and turns to this gun's ownership story. These are just the elements of which I am somewhat certain.

The grandson who sold the gun, his buddy who conspired in the sale, his buddy's father who perhaps unwittingly enabled the entire mess, and my brother each attempted to locate and retrieve the gun in those initial months without success. In exhausted frustration, each threw in the towel, assuming the gun was gone for good. I was not satisfied with that answer. Dad's gun belonged in our family. In my mind, chances were excellent that the gun existed somewhere. It surely had not been destroyed. I set my sights (pardon the pun) on getting Dad's gun back in time for his eightieth birthday, regardless of cost. Its reveal was to be my surprise gift to him.

While at times it seemed impossible, persistence paid off. Several months, many text messages, and a multitude of impassioned phone calls later, the gun was located and returned to Indiana for inspection. Up to that point, I had seen no pictures and had little more than the story of the father of the friend of the grandson who had sold the gun. I had no way of knowing if it was indeed Dad's gun or if the condition was similar to its condition from several years earlier. I needed to lay my eyes on the actual gun.

In what looked and felt like an illegal weapons exchange, I met the father of this grandson's friend in a dusty parking lot adjacent to the field where our youngest son was in the midst of a Little League baseball game. At the eleventh hour before this meeting, my opportunity to inspect and purchase the gun almost disappeared. The girlfriend of the purchaser's descendant, after having gone to the effort of locating the gun and returning it to Indiana, had become fearful of the review and the exchange. She had grown increasingly concerned that perhaps this commerce was illegal and that maybe the activity was being tracked or followed in some way. She nearly backed out to avoid potential trouble. Thankfully, she did not back out.

Much to my surprise and relief, it was indeed Dad's gun sitting right there before me on the passenger seat and floorboard of this man's truck. Except for a little inconsiderate handling, marginal maintenance, and a missing shoulder sling, it was also in good condition. Six hundred fifty dollars later, the gun was back in my safe with only a few days to spare before Dad's party.

His day arrived, sunny and beautiful. The farm was ready, and guests were staged along the gravel drive. Dad came rolling up to our farm's entrance, completely unaware of the surprise that awaited him. He was driven by one of his granddaughters so that he could focus on his surprise. Congratulations and high fives greeted him as they might a soldier returning to a hero's welcome. There were hugs, birthday wishes, greetings from friends not seen in years, and general merriment. Eventually, the hungry crowd settled for the blessing and an abundance of good food and fellowship. Even without the inspirational high point that was to come, by all measures, this celebration was a great event that resonated fondly with Dad and all his guests.

Back to the role guns played in the events of this special day. The secretive invitation sent months earlier encouraged whoever wanted to shoot clay pigeons to bring his gun(s) and ammo. Several did. Following lunch, Dad, in his Trackchair, motored out to the range to watch the action. After some time, with carefully contained excitement, and a more carefully contained shotgun, I retrieved the gun case from my vehicle and sat it down not far from Dad's spot. I positioned the closed case and a few boxes of ammo as if I, too, were preparing to join the collection of shooters. Before doing so, I stopped the shooting and motioned for everyone to come close.

Once the crowd was gathered and attentive, I explained that Dad had always been a skilled marksman but that it had been many years since he had last taken a shot at a clay pigeon. I introduced the fact that a long, tumultuous story existed about how his beloved gun had vanished several years earlier. I suggested that I would be happy to share more details of the unfortunate story with anyone interested but at a later time. This was the time to focus the crowd's attention squarely on Dad and some really good news. The good news that, should it be Dad's desire to shoot on this special day, it would be both *possible* and *fitting* for him to use his own beloved Remington 1100. I opened the case. He lit up.

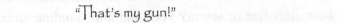

"That's my gun!"

DAD AND HIS 1100, TOGETHER AGAIN, 2017

I wouldn't trade that moment for much of anything. All the work was worth it. Dad beamed. Persistence pays.

The last time Dad had shot his gun was at least ten years earlier, probably more like fifteen years earlier for any repeated shooting or shooting at a moving target. It was before Mom died, before brain surgery, and before two surgeries on his left knee. It was before his right leg morphed into a boat anchor and before the tremors of Parkinson's disease and numerous medications to combat them. Dad would have been sixty-five or seventy years old and standing erect in an athletic stance. To be sure, it would have been a less challenging collection of conditions than from a seated position in a mobility chair compensating for the unpleasantries of Parkinson's in front of a large group of guests at the age of eighty.

When presented with the opportunity to shoot his gun once again, to my great delight and surprise, Dad responded,

"Yeah, I would kind of like to take my shot."

I loaded the gun and handed it back to him as the thrower was fitted with a clay pigeon. My camera was ready. All eyes were on Dad. All ears were listening for his command. "Pull!" The mechanical sound of the thrower slinging and rebounding lingered lonely in the otherwise hushed silence awaiting Dad's shot. It didn't take long. Pow! He destroyed the clay as he always had: one shot, one unrecognizable clay pigeon, pure dust. It wasn't a long shot or a lucky shot. It didn't take an eternity for him to aim and hit the bird just barely enough to consider it broken. Dad was locked on target almost immediately, and he turned it to dust with a picture-perfect shot.

After a short pause most certainly resulting from stunned disbelief, the audience erupted in cheer. Their reactions and body language almost audibly verbalized, "Did he actually just do that?" Dad smiled a proud, accomplished smile and handed the gun back to me.

SHOT HEARD 'ROUND THE FARM, 2017

Perhaps that will be Dad's last shot, perhaps not. Courage, resolve, confidence, skill, focus—Dad delivered in spades everything required in that moment.

> He left no room for Parkinson's or advancing years. He left no doubt.

I was fortunate enough to catch it on camera. The picture captures his steady, confident command of the gun, his eye still keenly focused on the clay, and the spent shell catapulted airborne out of the gun's automatic chamber through the lingering smoke. What a shot and what a great way to conclude Dad's eightieth birthday celebration with an exclamation point and a bang! Nice job, Dad!

In recent chapters, I've spoken briefly about Parkinson's, about multiple knee surgeries, about a large brain tumor, and about an uncooperative right leg. I have tried not to elaborate or dwell. Dad doesn't say much. Why should I? Dad was still driving himself around with some regularity until perhaps eighteen months ago. It was a tough decision for him to sell his car and self-impose additional restrictions, but Dad didn't complain on this point, either. He knew, tough as it was, that it was probably just the right thing to do. He still has his license and is certainly still able to drive, but I don't think he will. With children and grandchildren so close and so eager to help, he really doesn't need to drive.

Parkinson's disease makes it more difficult for Dad to write, so he looks to me a bit more for help with his checkbook and adjustments to wills, trusts, insurance policies, and legal documents. My sister cuts his hair, keeps up with his fashion, and helps in those areas where ladies tend to recognize need more readily. My brother also visits him often and takes him to appointments or out to jobsites, something Dad really enjoys. Sawyer visits him more than any other.

In the last eight years, Dad sold the home he and Mom built, moved briefly to a duplex in town, and then moved again to a nice independent-living facility just three miles from our home. We are fortunate that Dad lives close in such a nice place. His work ethic, his wisdom, and his prudent financial choices over so many years made retirement in such a nice place possible. We see Dad every few days and talk often by phone. On many Sundays after church, we join him for lunch and family fellowship. Whenever the mood strikes, we drop in for a quick visit and some ice cream just because we can. We enjoy his company on occasion while running errands. We host him at our homes on special days. We invite him to dance recitals and ball games. He still runs equipment and mows grass with the best of them if he's feeling up to transferring back and forth between seats. Dad has never met a puzzle he can't conquer and is usually the hand to beat at any card table.

Always generous, Dad created and funded a gifting trust to help all of his grandchildren as they move into seasons of life where they can use a boost. He has financed home improvements, real estate, and equipment purchases for my siblings and me. He often eats crackers, cereal, or spaghetti in his room and drinks water in order to save his meal allotment for visiting family. That's just who Dad is. We can shake our heads and ask that he not deprive himself all we want, but we know better than to hold our breath.

Dad never stops providing and caring for his family.
He chooses to be this sort of man every day.

PAPAW AND OUR BOYS HANGIN' ON OUR HEARTH, 2010

Dad has always been immensely popular with each and every one of his grandchildren—ten in total. Recently, yet another generation has developed who will look to him as the family patriarch. Dad has two great-grandchildren and perhaps others "in the oven." When our children were younger, he would push them for hours in the massive swing set he built from utility poles in his side yard. He would drive them around on the tractor, in the yard cart, or on a quad, snowmobile, or golf cart whenever possible. There were camping trips, visits to school, attendance at events and functions of all sorts, repairs of cherished toys, and breakfasts after church. To each of our children, and even to my wife, Dad is known simply as "Papaw." It is both a name and a term of endearment.

Our children had one other grandfather in their lives previously, at a distance. This man's example was quite different. Our kids never called their other grandfather "Grandpa" or anything similar. So different was his way and his example from Papaw's that our kids chose to call him

175

"Uncle" instead. By inclusion of this little tidbit, I mean no disrespect to uncles, and neither do our kids. I am an uncle many times over, and I take great pride in filling that role to the best of my ability. Rather, I think the juxtaposition of terms is revealing, perhaps even a touch humorous. It shows simply that, in the world of grandfathers, Papaw is loved and regarded on a plane with few others.

I want to be this kind of man for the loved ones in my life; I want to lead, love, and be loved sincerely at every stage. Such a privileged position cannot be demanded or purchased. It is the product of neither money nor skill nor excellence nor provision in any singular area. It is the fruit of genuine love and respect rooted in a lifetime of placing others before self. It is something difficult to describe but impossible to miss.

SIDEBAR 7:
SAWYER'S PLACE

While bonds are strong between Papaw and each of his grandchildren, none is tighter or stronger than the bond he has with his namesake, Sawyer Paul Geswein, our oldest child. Papaw and Sawyer have always been close. In recent years, their connection has grown tighter with each passing day. There are times when I think Sawyer has a stronger bond with Papaw than he has with me. In the midst of discipline, disagreement, or stress, I feel more certain of it. There could be far worse things. I take no offense. To have such a strong, grounded grandfather in his life to complement any influence Tekoa and I have can be nothing but positive.

PAPAW AND SAWYER IN THE BACK OF MY F-150, 2006

It would be proper to provide a bit more detail on the unique bond between these two men. Equally fitting are some additional reflections on Sawyer, this unique young man we named after my dad.

To say that Sawyer is a unique, intelligent, hardworking young man is a bit of an understatement. He is all these things and more, a character from every angle. Certainly not perfect, Sawyer is a fine young man making his way in a positive direction.

Sawyer has always loved mowing grass and other outdoor manual labor from his earliest days, just like me, just like Papaw. Sawyer spent many hours on my lap at the helm of mowers and tractors well before he could walk or talk. He started mowing solo at six years old, first with a mechanical reel mower, then onto a small family riding mower whose pedals he was not able to reach. I would get him started in a big, safe area free of trees or obstructions and let him go. Lap after lap he would go. He knew to keep his hands and feet out of harm's way, he knew how to disengage the blades, and he knew to get up from the seat whenever he needed to stop—*before* he needed to stop. Later, he bought his own equipment: a modern push mower with an internal combustion engine and a quirky but beloved Honda riding mower. The Honda comes with a leadership example of its own, which is part of a story that is interesting enough to include.

Sawyer first came to know and love this Honda on the farm we now own. At the time, both the Honda and the farm were owned by our good friends the Bracketts. Sawyer's interest in this mower reached a point where he badly wanted to buy it and launch his mowing business as a proud Honda owner. I asked the Bracketts about their plans for the mower. It was seldom used, and they appeared to have little sentimental attachment to it. I also informed them of Sawyer's interest and intentions. The Honda was a high-quality but peculiar mower, a perfect match for Sawyer. I insisted— and Sawyer agreed—that if he really wanted the mower, he needed to approach Dr. Brackett properly with his request, small man to big man. He needed to explain his interest in purchasing the mower for his business and ask Dr. Brackett if he would be willing to sell.

Sawyer went into the conversation prepared to pay as much as one hundred fifty of his hard-earned dollars. Following Dr. Brackett's willingness to sell, Sawyer proceeded to ask how much money he would need to complete the transaction. Dr. Brackett reflected pensively, appeared to mentally compute, and came back to Sawyer with his suggestion: one dollar. I contained my amusement beneath a serious, contemplative look of my own. Sawyer turned toward me with the widest, most astonished, most excited look on his young face. Four quarters, a proper handshake, and some appreciative smiles later, Sawyer had his first genuine riding mower, a Honda.

SAWYER WITH HIS HONDA RIDER AND SUPPORT EQUIPMENT, 2010

Of all times and places, this memorable event and transaction took place at the funeral home during the closing stages of Mom's celebration of life. Somehow, that seems strangely fitting, the Bracketts living and teaching beyond currency in a way that churned celebration from sadness in the heart of a driven young man.

I think my mother was smiling right then, maybe even to the point of releasing an unintended snort she was known to emit when particularly tickled by something. Well played, Dr. Brackett, well played. That was a very nice gesture and a great learning experience. Thank you!

With that purchase, at the tender age of seven, Sawyer officially launched his lawn-care business. Equally fitting was the fact that Sawyer tended first to the lawn of his great-grandmother (Mom's mom) and then to the lawns of a few friends or neighbors.

In generations past, such spirit and drive would have been celebrated. In modern culture, however, Sawyer's pursuits, and our encouragement of them, drew criticism, particularly in those early years. How irresponsible of us to allow our young child to operate dangerous machinery! We received a letter in the mail from a friend of our neighbor. From our neighbor's garage only a short distance away, this man had watched young Sawyer honing his craft in our own yard and was deeply concerned. He didn't take the few steps between properties to address his concerns head-on; rather, he stated his concerns in a letter and distanced himself by way of the U. S. Postal Service.

Our response politely acknowledged his letter and his concern but resolutely stated our enduring, bolder, more traditional approach. I recall its wording being something like the following: "We raise our children toward work ethic, life skills, and good judgment. We teach them about risk and having respect for equipment and elements of life that can do them harm. We will not change our approach, though we thank you kindly for your concern. In our humble opinions,

> Ignorance, sloth, poor judgment, poor health, and ineptitude are common outcomes of bubble-wrapped isolation on life's sidelines.

These represent far greater risks than physical injury from properly maintained machinery operated skillfully by a young person with a brain and a sense of self-preservation."

We didn't hear back from our neighbor's friend.

We've had doors closed in our faces and experienced rejection in several forms. Through it all, Sawyer and his business have grown and improved. At age eight, Sawyer's business was formalized into an official limited liability company (LLC). He grows his business steadily each year based on reliable, honest, and good-quality work at fair prices. Sawyer has grown in size, judgment, and aptitude. Trimmers, edgers, blowers, snow-removal tools, chainsaws, and other equipment and services have been added.

In the spring of 2017, at age fourteen, a local television news station, WLFI, did a nice story on Sawyer, his business, and his aspirations. We happily accept the backlash and the risks of championing and challenging our children at young ages in exchange for personal development and growth of this sort. Thank you, WLFI. Well done, Sawyer.

In August 2017, Sawyer turned fifteen and received his learner's permit to drive. New opportunities opened, thanks in large part once again to Papaw. Though Papaw's mobility prevented him from helping Sawyer directly with most physical tasks, his willingness to ride along and sit patiently in the truck at each of Sawyer's jobs meant that Sawyer could expand his business more quickly. A full twelve months earlier than expected, Sawyer was able to expand his business beyond areas he could reach by foot. Good ole Papaw—always willing to help.

PAPAW AND SAWYER WITH SAWYER'S FIRST
TRUCK, DECEMBER 24, 2017

In preparation for the summer of 2018, Sawyer resolved to buy his first truck and a proper landscape trailer to more efficiently move from job to job. Papaw found just the right truck from someone in his retirement complex. Papaw went with Sawyer to purchase it the day before Christmas 2017. Papaw also traveled to southern Indiana with Sawyer early that following spring as he checked out and purchased a nice, new landscape trailer. The summer of 2018 was a Papaw/Sawyer traveling road show. Those two were always together, always enjoying and appreciating each other, always bonding and making money.

Today, at age eighteen, with two trucks, four mowers, multiple trimmers, blowers, a commercial aerator, and sundry equipment, Sawyer is able to drive himself and his business wherever he wants to go. He no longer needs Papaw or me to be physically in the passenger seat. Along with Sawyer's freedom and independence comes a confidence that everyone who loves Sawyer shares. He'll make mistakes, just as Papaw did and just as I do, but his foundation is strong, and his trajectory is positive.

What place does Sawyer's story really have in this book of reflections? Why do I include a sidebar unique to him? There are several reasons.

Sawyer is our first child. Speaking as a proud father, I'll add that he is also my first son. He occupies a unique position. Since he is our first child, we cut our parental teeth with him. I have made many mistakes raising him, more than I have made with our next two children. Such is a familiar story and progression as parents and children learn and grow together. Thankfully, Tekoa and I have also done many things well in our parenting. Where mistakes or gaps existed, Papaw has been available to encourage and shore things up—always.

Sawyer and Papaw reflect each other in many ways and are as tight as any grandfather and grandson can be. This book would be incomplete if I failed to elaborate on their bond, this enviable continuity of spirit, blood, and family.

Finally, Sawyer is vested in this book. He started this journey of discovery and writing with me back in 2015. He and our other children have followed its progress with some interest ever since.

I reflect fondly on that first trip back to Sawyer's roots in South Carolina. It was November 2015, and Sawyer was barely thirteen years old. It was just the two of us in a rented Hyundai, enjoying freedom, crisp air, and purpose. We were headed south to see Bob, Charles, King and Augusta, Orrin Hudson, and others. We sought to enjoy and listen to them, to learn more about their own lives and motivations as I prepared to write. We needed to connect some dots in the eleven years of life lived since these folks had last seen Sawyer. We visited Stone Mountain. We laughed. We ate. We rode mountain bikes. We strategized comical ways to rid our lawn of moles, and we flogged that poor Hyundai up the mountain to Highlands, North Carolina. Sawyer was introduced to parts of my life he had never known. He sampled boiled peanuts and enjoyed a waterfall we could drive under. It was a great and memorable trip.

In November 2015, the book had few words, no form, and no title, much less a subtitle. Just a few months later, February 2016, a subtitle began taking shape in a memorable way as I was compelled to write a letter of appreciation to Sawyer.

Perhaps best understanding comes by reading this letter for yourself.

18 Feb 16   1/3

Dear Sawyer,

As I was doing dishes this evening following dinner and overheard Momma asking if you had homework, I was suddenly struck with the need to tell you how proud I am of you and *the* fine young man you *are* becoming. To Momma's question, I casually turned to witness the scene play out as I fully expected it would. You politely responded, "a little bit" as you strolled past toward your room, already in mid-stride; our responsible young 13-year no longer needing monitoring for such things. Even now as I write, my prideful grin stretches slightly as I listen to the partially muffled sound of tuba practice now that homework must be finished... Not TV or video games, or net-surfing, but homework and tuba. Combine these positive realities with the glowing report your Uncle Shawn felt compelled to give me following your helping him with chainsaw and fencerow

(OVER)

LETTER TO SAWYER, PAGE 1, 2016

2/3

work earlier this week. It is so nice, and becoming so common, to hear reports like these from people who are just so impressed and hopeful after spending time with you.

Someday I hope you get to experience this same sort of pride as your children develop

I started writing just as soon as the idea hit me; partially because I wanted to capture these thoughts for you while they were fresh, but also, (you'll be happy to know) because I believe we may have struck upon the title and direction for our book ... <u>The Man You Are Becoming</u>. I really like it, more than any idea I've had thus far ... kind of like The Holy Moly ☺. It'll be a book about Jesus, and Grandpa Geswein, and Papaw, and Zig Ziglar, and John Wooden, and Professor Bob, and Charles Fridy, and Teddy Roosevelt, and Jim Rohn, and, and, and many others I've been blessed to learn from. It'll be a book about fatherhood

LETTER TO SAWYER, PAGE 2, 2016

(continued)   18 Feb 16   3/3

and mentorship and leading by example. About
the perfection of Jesus and our pursuit of his example
in spite of ourselves. About surrounding ourselves
with, and learning from, men of character, courage,
and honor who themselves have shared and formed
our values. It will be about honoring and thanking
those men while there is still time, overlooking
vices and building on virtues. It will be about
the men we are becoming.

So, I conclude where I began, happy and
hopeful. Happy and filled with pride that you are
my boy and thankful that you are on a fantastic
path filled with hope and promise and contribution.
I am so glad you are my boy and I'll work
hard to be the best father I can be for you just
as Papaw has been for me. Have a great day
at school today. Love &
                        Prayers,
                                Daddy ☺

LETTER TO SAWYER, PAGE 3, 2016

I had this letter waiting for him to find before school the following morning. It is an important piece of the puzzle. I'm so glad I wrote this letter to him. As I look back, comparing its words of intention to what this book has actually become over seventy thousand words later, I'm pleased to say I think we stayed pretty well on track.

As Sawyer's story and this sidebar unfold, I would be remiss not to take several steps back and appreciate one of the wonderful educators who played a *huge* part in setting Sawyer up for success in life and academics. Sawyer's first days of kindergarten were a train wreck. This statement is not an exaggeration. He was headed for academic disaster. I attended a welcome meeting for parents in the day or two prior to his first day of kindergarten. I left the meeting apprehensive at best, fearful at worst. His assigned teacher bored me to death and had so little structure and focus to her talk that my interest and attention left the room within minutes. I remained physically in place but in considerable agony for the remainder of her presentation. I feared that Sawyer, being much like me, would have the same reaction. He did. It wasn't good.

Within days, Tekoa and I were in meetings with school administrators. Sawyer was engaged in behavioral assessments, and we were encouraged to consider special classes and ADHD drugs. Seriously, the suggestion of medication arose in less than a week from school administrators and from a locally known doctor who *hadn't even seen Sawyer personally*. What a cop-out! He didn't need special classes, and he certainly didn't need drugs. He was a high-functioning child who needed a structured, firm classroom along with the love and guidance of a great teacher. Tekoa was wise enough to have already been scouting other kindergarten teachers. She saw in Mrs. Stockton the right combination. To the credit of school administrators, they supported the move, and the switch was made in short order.

In that *very first day* with Mrs. Stockton, Sawyer's academic future changed. He thrived with Mrs. Stockton's firm but caring direction. She established Sawyer's positive academic path, and he never departed from it. In January 2021, a semester earlier than most of his classmates, Sawyer graduated from high school with the highest of honors while on the most rigorous academic track, having received only two Bs in all his years of middle and high school. That's nearly a straight 4.0!

We are incredibly proud of him and so thankful for Mrs. Stockton and a handful of other teachers who really helped along the way. Sawyer and Mrs. Stockton remain close. In fact, Mrs. Stockton was Sawyer's confirmation sponsor at church in April 2018. Tekoa was absolutely right; Mrs. Stockton, you were a godsend. Thank you! Our world needs more teachers like you, just as it needs more fathers like mine.

Following Sawyer's sidebar and its closing paragraphs about the positive influence of a strong, caring teacher, I conclude this entire chapter with a heartfelt message to faithful, conservative parents and educators. We know you are out there, and we appreciate you. I suspect at times you feel as if you are fighting an unwinnable war. You are not. Parents like us and conservative folks spanning generations are behind you, supporting the important work you do. We recognize that the job before you is difficult, and we appreciate the fact that you take it on as you do.

Young people are our future.

As we know all too well, unfortunately, the examples and materials with which children are presented today often lean heavily left by design. Liberals control much of the mainstream media, and they do everything in their power to force their agenda upon young people constantly. CNN 10, formerly CNN Student News, is readily available in schools and has been since 1989 for a reason. Does Fox or any other outlet with right-leaning bias enjoy or pursue such broad coverage? No. Credit the left with forethought and strategy in this area; they are not passive. These folks know full well the truth of the following statement, most often attributed to Jim Morrison, and they are using it to advance their agenda: "Whoever controls the media, controls the mind."

Conservatives, traditionalists, Christians, others of faith, and supporters of the nuclear family, we must wake up to what is going on and get to work boldly defending our children and our beliefs. Conservative educators who've had enough of the bias and the agenda pressure, please hear me clearly. We want you—we desperately need you—to take back your classrooms and stand up for what you believe, regardless of the stack of prescribed fecal matter you may be required to distribute.

It is your classroom, and you are in charge. Your role and your influence start in the classroom, but they extend well beyond.

If a particularly liberal teacher can decorate her entire room in misappropriated rainbow colors and audaciously populate her desk with pictures of her wife while threatening conservative students with expulsion for sharing their conservative views during classroom "debates," then you certainly can personalize your classroom and your teaching approach to reflect your own values. It is your classroom, and this is still a free country. As you might imagine, this colorful example is quite real. We've actually lived that one and several more of the same sort.

These days, there seems to be no room for debate. If you don't agree with the liberal agenda, you are wrong, nothing but an uneducated hater. It is a familiar and interesting conclusion from those who espouse acceptance and advertise open minds.

> Administrators can limit and dictate some things,
> but they cannot control your substance, and
> they cannot diminish your influence.

You don't need to hide your faith or pretend it is not important to you. You are not forced to endure vulgarity, vaping, distractive clothing, and disrespectful behavior in your classroom. Is CNN 10 really necessary? Perhaps you can open a topic for real debate and critical thought according to your personal lead and not that of some agenda-sponsored broadcaster.

> Your students need your strong, faithful example.

They want and need to know who you really are if you expect them to learn from you, if you want them to follow you. You are faithful and creative. Your classroom can be, too. Lord knows the other side is doing everything it can to exert its will and champion its causes. Please be strong, courageous, and proactive. John Stuart Mill, ironically a classical liberal, first stated way back in 1867, "Bad men need nothing more to compass their ends, than that good men should look on and do nothing." His words are just as relevant today as they were more than a hundred fifty years ago. Perhaps now they are even more relevant as their application extends equally to women. Love our kids enough to do what is best for them while staying just this side of trouble so that you can keep doing what you are doing.

> Our kids need you!

CHAPTER 15

CHOOSING FAITHFUL VICTORY

Lessons on Daily Choices, Manning One's Station,
My Friend Matt, and Saying Goodbye

IT IS A GREAT SOURCE OF PRIDE AND ENCOURAGEMENT TO WATCH DAD
live his life as a victor rather than a victim. He does the best he can, no
matter his circumstances, without complaint. Dad grieves Mom's loss and
the loss of many of his physical strengths and aptitudes, but he doesn't
dwell. He doesn't openly lament the crosses with which he's been laden.
His typical response to each new challenge is

"It's okay; it's what we've got to do."

With faithful spirit and peace, gratitude, perhaps, for the good stuff,
and tolerance of the bad, Dad simply lives out God's mysterious plan
for his life one day at a time. Jesus's own agony-strained words from the
Garden of Gethsemane ring eerily similar. His were words of patient,
obedient acceptance of His Father's plan:

"Not my will but yours be done."

(Luke 22:42)

Several pages ago, just before describing Dad's popularity with his grandchildren and his unique bond with Sawyer, I mentioned that Dad "chooses" to be the way that he is. Being a certain way, at least in attitude and spirit, is indeed a choice. We are not able to choose many things, not our parents, our families, our genders, our sizes and shapes, and certainly not our crosses. Still, in keeping with God's plan, by our daily choices of attitude and action, we determine the vibrancy of our life's tapestry, the hues and textures it impresses upon others.

Our daily choices make us.

I choose to follow the vast majority of examples and lessons Dad and others have provided and continue to provide. I have chosen to abandon a fractional few and to tweak others to my interpretation of what is optimal. I am not my father. That's okay. I feel neither inferior nor superior to him. I feel grateful, appreciative, and complementary. I proudly choose to be my father's son. I choose to emulate him in many ways. Dad may never write a book, and I may never sell crop insurance. Together, we've done both.

Together we are stronger and more complete
than we could ever be alone.

Pope John Paul II was one of Dad's favorite popes—mine, too. He died in the same year as my grandfather, 2005. I remember Pope John Paul II reasonably well, particularly the later years of his life as his health was failing. He was at his station until the very end. He was a popular and widely respected Pope with great influence over his pontificate of nearly thirty years. It was never reported that Pope John Paul II complained under the stresses and strains of his position or bemoaned his failing health. He stood firm in his faith and for those things in which he believed deeply. He survived an assassination attempt in 1981. Upon recovery, he proceeded to meet with his would-be assassin in prison and offer him forgiveness. Pope John Paul II was an inspirational leader and a guidepost for many, including Dad and me.

While neither my dad nor any of the men or women who've held place in this chronicle can boast of life experiences so large and public as those of

Pope John Paul II, the wisdom, leadership, and elements of self they have shared are every bit as positive and influential on a local level.

I once heard it said that Pope John Paul II taught us not only how to live but also how to die, holding fast to his purpose with dignity to the very end. Stated more casually, as in the feel-good man movie *Secondhand Lions*, Pope John Paul II "went out with his boots on."

I don't want my dad or any of these folks to die—ever. Regardless, we will all die. We know not our hour. Are we ready? Have we manned our stations well and contributed according to the gifts given and opportunities presented to us? I hope so. Such should be our aims. I bring this portion of my book to a close with the sincerest of thanks to Dad and to each of the impactful men and women mentioned here. You have contributed to me. You have influenced me in so many positive ways. I am deeply grateful. I hope this message is received in time for each of you to absorb my appreciation fully. Thank you!

Honorable Mention

MATT AND I, PREPARED TO EMBARK ON ANOTHER TRIP, 2011

It is impossible to be thoroughly thankful and bring these reflections current without mentioning my good friend Matt. At so many points along this reflective journey, I could have introduced Matt and diverted onto tangents of our friendship and the fruit it has borne. In this book, I prefer instead to provide just the helicopter view for now.

Matt and I met some twenty-six years ago in an onboarding classroom for folks newly hired at Michelin. Each of us was getting started with his first postcollege job—full-time, no-joke, career-genesis job. Matt was diving into manufacturing engineering, and I was headed toward on-vehicle development engineering, test driving. Like me, Matt is a car guy, a Porsche fan mostly. He had great parents and a spirit of adventure.

Besides cars and engineering, we shared interests in cycling and attractive females. Bringing the latter interests together, we concocted a grand notion of assembling a group of Michelin new hires on a beautiful fall weekend and pedaling our way across the better part of South Carolina. None of the attractive females on our lists came forward for the adventure. Matt's charm must have been just as good as mine at the time, meaning not good at all. Even though the ladies snubbed us, we decided to venture out anyway, just the two of us. That first trip across South Carolina in 1995 started a tradition and kindled a friendship of great value that continues today.

At the time of this writing, Matt and I have covered well over five thousand miles together through thirty-six of the great states of this land. Matt is on his fourth bike; I'm still on my original trusty old Trek 930. Our annual bicycle adventure has connected us for twenty-four trips spanning twenty-five years. Between us, we have more than forty years of marriage to the same wonderful women each of us started with. We have been blessed with three great kids each—five boys and one girl in total. Matt and I have both lost our mothers but, thankfully, still treasure great fathers. Our families have each experienced miscarriages, multiple job changes and challenges, moves from here to there, and the highs and lows that are a natural part of marriage, parenthood, and life.

Over all these years, all this family, all this life, Matt has been a true friend to me, sharing company with Brian and few others. I am very grateful. Thank you, Matt, for being such a good friend. I'm fortunate to have you in my tightest circle. I look forward to our next fourteen states, our concluding trip from coast to coast, and the many chunks of life we are sure to encounter and share along the way. Perhaps our adventures may someday form the backbone of another book, this one of friendship; of adventure; of life shared; of raising kids, loving wives, and doing our best to live in a way our kids want to follow. Whatever it may be, my friend, it will be a pleasure sharing it with you.

In Memory of...

It takes time to write, rewrite, illustrate, and publish a book, particularly when it is not one's full-time job. Before now, I had no appreciation for how much time. In such a span of months and years, life continues uninterrupted for most folks. For others, perhaps life stops somewhere in the midst. Life happens in all moments, regardless of books. It happens in spite of face creams, liposuction, lifts, and tucks. Life happens in spite of our most fervent prayers that hardship and death should pass our loved ones by.

To be sure, we will all die at the end of some measure of life and contribution.

Bob did, King did, and Augusta did, too. I am eternally grateful that God saw fit to bless my life with theirs. I am a better man for having known each of them.

On July 6, 2020, Albert King Dixon II died somewhat unexpectedly at the age of eighty-three after a short bout with pancreatic cancer. Little more than five weeks later, in the dark of night, peaceful sleep morphed into joyful journey as Augusta, too, was welcomed home. I did not get to say a proper farewell to King and Augusta, but I'm thankful to have been able to visit them in January 2020 to catch up and share the first manuscript of this book. I was able to thank them personally for their cherished friendship and their positive influence on my life and that of my young family. Finer people cannot be found. The good Dixon name and legacy of service will be praised for generations in the state of South Carolina.

In the days and hours before Bob's passing on February 4, 2020, the good Lord arranged and blessed our final earthly visit. Of this fact, I am certain, just as certain as I am that God allowed me to be with Grandpa Geswein as he drew his final breath on earth. There are lessons in each of these events that God wanted to teach *me*. Perhaps, too, there was something in my presence during their final moments that God wanted to express to each of *them*. Perhaps something like this:

Thank you, dear child. On this one, too, you had an impact.
Well done, my good and faithful servant. Welcome home!

I hadn't seen Bob since 2015, though I tried on several occasions. On one particular occasion in 2019, I even stopped by with our two sons as we passed through Clemson on a spring-break adventure. We tried unsuccessfully to reach him over and over and over again in the days leading up to our visit. On the particular evening that we arrived in town, we stopped at his home and knocked loudly on the front door since we knew he was hard of hearing. Our knocking at the front door didn't raise him, so we added some percussion at the back door, close to where he always sat in his chair. Sieger even stretched and strained to peer into a few elevated windows. "Bob, it's Spencer!" I announced at considerable volume. Still, nothing raised him. Though we felt sure he was inside, with no positive response, we left.

Days later, we learned that Bob had indeed been inside. He had heard only enough of our racket to be alarmed and to call his dearest friend, Serji, for backup. We were already gone by the time Serji arrived. We were saddened that we had missed another opportunity to visit Bob and saddened further when we learned that we had startled him and caused him stress; that certainly was not our intention.

Fast-forward to mid-January 2020. Work took me to Charlotte on several occasions, just a short drive from Clemson. Bob was to celebrate ninety-six years of life on January 24. I wanted to celebrate with him, to see him, to share my gratitude and my manuscript. I wanted to read a bit of the first copy of this manuscript with him. God had urged, and Dad's familiar guidance had resonated with me several weeks earlier: "That's good enough. Finish the manuscript and connect with Bob right away. You can fix the little stuff later." After more than four years of work, I stuck a fork in the first manuscript on January 18 and made arrangements through Serji to visit Bob on his actual ninety-sixth birthday, January 24, 2020, with a copy of the manuscript in hand.

The door opened to Bob's quiet home on that cloudy Thursday afternoon. Bob looked peaceful, then filled to the brim with surprise and joy at my visit. It was so nice to see him again, such a kind man. Serji and Bob's other visitors knew Bob's time on earth was drawing to a close. I relished my time with him. I told him how nice it was to see him again, how thankful I was for his love and leadership in my life. I told him that I had *finally* completed the manuscript I had been working on about manhood, about my dad, and about him. Bob was so genuinely pleased. It wasn't his inclusion in these reflections that pleased him so; rather, it was that I had completed this project. He knew that it was a project of considerable importance to me and that I was happy. He was happy for me and proud.

BOB WITH MY FIRST MANUSCRIPT ON HIS NINETY-
SIXTH BIRTHDAY, JANUARY 30, 2020

He held the manuscript in his hands for a time, though I'm not sure how much of it he could see, much less read. His glasses didn't even seem to sit squarely on his face. I turned for him to some key pages and pointed to some memory-stirring pictures. We rekindled those memories and shared some labored laughs. Seeing the picture of himself with the Porsche from our trip to the mountains and reflecting on that experience caused him to silently mouth his familiar phrase "My soul and body!" Picturing him mouthing those words still brings a smile to my face.

I read to him some of the passages that I believed to be more impactful, passages I wanted him to hear. I wanted. I wanted. Thankfully, rather than completely dominating our precious time, I also listened carefully to his final few words. They came slowly. It was difficult for him to speak, but speak he did.

"Keep doing your work. What we give returns. This world is hard. People are too worldly. I look forward."

His final sentence seemed to linger. Was it a complete thought, or did he suspend it by design for me to connect it to something secure? Not long after sharing these thoughts, Bob appeared tired and in need of a break. We took a photo or two. I gave him a careful embrace and closed with words similar to those he had so often directed to me: "Love and prayers, Bob. Love and prayers. Thank you, my friend. Bye-bye."

I was privileged to visit with Bob this one final time in good condition and in good spirits before his heavenly journey. Five days after our visit, the good Lord took Bob home. Serji shared with me that only a handful of hours following my visit, quality visiting opportunities had passed.

Please understand that I hadn't seen Bob in more than four years despite numerous attempts. I had printed the full 160-page manuscript for the first time barely seventy-two hours prior to our final visit because something powerful had told me to hustle. I was able to visit Bob in his final hours of peaceful clarity on his ninety-sixth birthday because the work I love had brought me to the region, and my schedule was flexible enough to allow the visit. The forty-five minutes I enjoyed with Bob were forty-five precious minutes of the last hour or two he had available for quality visits. God took Bob home five days later.

Please don't believe this all happened by chance. Don't be deceived. Don't believe that the alignment of these events was coincidental. It was no more coincidental than the divine instruction and my obedience that had brought me to my grandfather's side—the only person at his side—literally for the final five minutes of his life. We make our plans, and we do our best, but all of this is far beyond us.

Despite our illusions of power and brilliance, we are not in control.

Whether we believe it now or not, we will each face death and truth. We will face the fact that there is a brilliant, benevolent Creator and Director of all we think we see and know. We can choose to ignore it if we wish, only to our detriment. Random explosions and mutations do not create human beings, fish, trees, planets, toenails, pupils, echo location, guanine crystals, and cockroaches by undirected coincidence.

God *created* according to His plan and His providence. Our time on earth is short, and His is the direction and the kingdom to seek first. The only things that are eternal are the things we do for Him. "Keep doing your work. What we give returns." What an interesting and appropriate choice of concluding thoughts. Bob's measure of life and contribution was considerable. I am grateful to have been a part of it.

Is it any surprise that, some months after Bob's passing, an envelope arrived at my home from an attorney's office with a letter stating that Bob had remembered me in the distribution of his estate? As he did for a considerable number of people, Bob shared his time, his talent, and his treasure. By example, he taught each of us to do the same for others. Such a kind and generous teacher—Bob's legacy continues. Rest in peace, my friend.

I cannot close this message and fail to acknowledge Serji, a friend and indirect mentor I've come to know through Bob. Surprisingly, I recall meeting Serji only a few times prior to Bob's final chapter of life. I've traded text messages with him on a number of occasions and have spoken with him by phone just a few more times. I've heard a great deal about him over the last twenty-five years, however, and I am fortunate to have witnessed the excellence of his life through his friendship and service to Bob. Thank you, Serji. You, your wife, and your family are the most committed and genuine of friends. I've been watching.

CHAPTER 16

CRUSADING

Making Lists, Molding Men, Joining Forces,
and Driving Action toward the Finish

WE COME NOW TO A POINT OF SUMMARY, A POINT REQUIRING RESOLVE
and commitment to positive action. Much has been shared in these stories
and examples. We have been reminded of many things admirable: kindness,
courage, virtue, honor, strength, resolve, commitment, consideration,
generosity, compassion, discipline, pride in one's work, value in one's word,
and the gumption to strive unceasingly for what's right and true.

Dad and my crew have done—and continue to do—their parts. What
about us? What role does each of us fill in this, the grandest of plays? What
restorative actions are you and I going to take in this world desperate for truth,
leadership, and healing? How are we to leave this place better than we found it,
enriching the lives of others in the process? How are you going to make yourself,
your family, your _____ better? What are you actually going to *do*?

The year 2020 was a bizarre, almost unbelievable year. So many things
have happened since I completed the first manuscript on January 18,
2020. In March, our world withdrew into its proverbial shell in fear of the
COVID-19 virus, fear and reaction both enormously overblown, in my
personal opinion. Who knows how long government leaders will "require"
that we hold a fetal position? How long will we listen and comply? In May,
George Floyd was killed without cause, and the nation erupted in ways

both productive and not. We wore our masks and carried our differences to the polls in November and still can't emerge with a president the country respects. The year 2020 goes into the books as a mess!

Without going down into many possible rabbit holes, I'll just say that *all* lives matter. Evil comes in all colors, shapes, sizes, and political parties. It comes wrapped in uniforms, baggy jeans, pressed suits, hoodies, lab coats, cowboy hats, and, yes, even in church clothes. We are all human, sons and daughters of God. There are bad apples in every barrel, but that doesn't make every barrel bad. We are really all in one barrel anyway, aren't we? We all trace our DNA back to the same parents. We all inhabit the same earthly home. We all have equal share in heavenly promise. We are brothers and sisters, all flawed, all flavored, and all prejudiced to one degree or another by our individual experiences.

Yes, we are different—duh! We don't have to pretend that we are exactly the same, and we don't have to hate on each other because of our differences. In his most memorable address to the Atlanta Exposition in 1895, Booker T. Washington stated brilliantly, "In all things that are purely social we can be as separate as the fingers, yet one as the hand in all things essential to mutual progress." Can't we all just acknowledge that each and every one of us is a beloved and priceless child of God? Can't we all just act as though we truly believe this to be true and treat each other accordingly? Here again we find perfect application of the Golden Rule, do unto others as you would have them do unto you.

So, to repeat, how are you going to make yourself,
your family, your _____ better?
What are you actually going to do?

I hope you will be driven beyond reflection and good intention. I trust that you will struggle earnestly forward with actions and gestures like those you've read about from Dad and my crew. I hope some will stop procrastinating. Stop getting caught up in getting caught up and attend to those truly important things that need to be done right now. Perhaps more than a few will be led to thank and appreciate the positive people in their own lives, to strive today and every new day to contribute more positively to the lives of others. I hope that still others will grab the reins of their lives and finally charge with gusto after whatever it is God has called them to be and to do. Perhaps these stories of regular folks with regular lives having uncommon influence will compel us to believe that each of us is, in fact, a carefully crafted, treasured child of God with his own unique gifts to be developed and shared for His glory. I hope you truly grasp and internalize the fact that time is short—not as an excuse to lose hope but rather as a reason to get busy.

I don't know if I am called to be an author or motivator of any sort. I would like to think that perhaps I am. This fond notion has rattled around in my head for some time as I've pursued whatever other things have been needed to provide for my family. What I do know is that I am doing my part to make a way for writing and speaking. I am putting in the work.

I am standing in the arena.

I finally finished this book, expressed the gratitude I needed to express, and stated my position on matters of importance. I have placed myself in a better position to answer God's call when it comes. In this moment, I am reminded of and encouraged by the wonderful speech excerpt from President Theodore Roosevelt entitled "The Man in the Arena." Perhaps you've not heard it, or perhaps there may be some benefit in reading it once again.

> It is not the critic who counts; not the man who points out how the strong man stumbles, or where the doer of deeds could have done them better. The credit belongs to the man who is actually in the arena, whose face is marred by dust and sweat and blood; who strives valiantly; who errs, who comes short again and again, because there is no effort without error and shortcoming; but who does actually strive to do the deeds; who knows great enthusiasms, the great devotions; who spends himself in a worthy cause; who at the best knows in the end the triumph of high achievement, and who at the worst, if he fails, at least fails while daring greatly, so that his place shall never be with those cold and timid souls who neither know victory nor defeat. —Theodore Roosevelt, April 23, 1910

In addition to getting on with this book, what else does *my* commitment to action look like? Here are some things that have come to mind in recent days. The list is not exhaustive, and it may not be in proper order. Does either of these concerns really matter? Time, urgent needs, and varying levels of progress and fulfillment may drive me to alter my list. I fully expect it. You should, too. I'm not trying to boil the ocean, and I'm not going to succumb to analysis paralysis. I'm just going to get about these few important things that are immediately before me and keep moving forward.

1. Share, improve, and promote this book and *act* on its lessons.
2. Champion manliness in young men and fight emasculation in our culture.
3. Lead more camps for young men and get help to develop myself and this program further, ultimately reaching larger groups of young men and their families.
4. Help coach our son's athletic team(s).
5. Develop a deeper, more genuine relationship with God that more effectively directs my thoughts and actions.
6. Love my wife more completely, as Jesus loved the Church. Work harder on our relationship, understanding that she is different from me by God's design with her own needs and desires that are equally important to my own. Complement her and help her become the woman God is calling her to be.
7. Encourage and enrich our children more. Nag less.
8. Listen more intently and serve others more purely.
9. Think less about myself, my needs, and my hurts. Turn attention instead outwardly toward others who have troubles far greater than my own.
10. Get up—no "Snooze"!

It's my list. It's enough for now. Listing more at this hour probably only adds stress and distraction and wastes precious time. If I make real progress in each of the areas listed, I'll be far better off than I am today.

Please make your own list. Please do it right now. Don't delay and don't fret over making it perfect or complete.

I've left a few pages at the back of the book blank for you. Just grab a pencil and do it. Your list need not be more elaborate than this, but please write it down and refer to it often with sincerity and commitment. You'll be glad you did. We will all be glad you did.

A few of the actions at the top of my list require elaboration, starting with Point 1, this book. I typed the final few words of its first draft on Saturday, January 18, 2020. Minor tweaks followed, and a few trusted friends began reading it almost immediately. I finished the second manuscript in August 2020 in the midst of global idiocy. More proofreading and improvement came with the third version. I signed with a publisher in late November and submitted my manuscript for their scrutiny within days of my fiftieth birthday, in December. Before you is the finished product. I finished my book. With your help I trust, I am promoting it to others. Yes, most days I do well to *act* on the lessons this book contains and many more. It's a struggle. Some days I fail miserably. I'm a *long* way from perfect, but I keep "hoeing in that direction," as my friend and first editor, Andrea, suggested in her foreword.

Point 2, the emasculation of men in our culture, is a burr in my saddle. I despise it, and I actively fight against it. It serves no purpose but to weaken individuals and society. I hope this book encourages more men, more women, and more families to champion masculinity and male leadership without apology and to do so as actively as we encourage confident development of women toward their highest and best selves. Our country was built by strong, courageous men and women of faith. Should we forsake strength, courage, faith, the concept of male and female together as one, then the structure our families and our societies will fall out of balance to the detriment of our nation and our world. In days gone by, men such as Booker T. Washington, Teddy Roosevelt, John Wooden, Charles Ingalls, my father, and characters of their stature influenced generations of both men and women in a positive way. Men strove toward biblical manhood, and women saw what they should expect from a man of God. Women, too, sought to fulfill God's purpose for their lives.

Some readers may be coming to a boil with this topic, misconstruing my words to conclude that I am somehow against women or filled with misogyny and homophobia. Such conclusions are simply not true.

I love women, just as I love my neighbors and myself. I have many treasured women in my life, and I want nothing but the best for them. Why on earth would I want anything less? To a significant degree, it's my love of, and respect for, women that prompts me to put forth my call for masculinity. Men and women are not the same. This should not come as a surprise. I believe men and women have been fashioned to complement and complete, not so much to compete. Life is better for the women in my life when I am being the best man that I can be according to God's template. Life is also better for me, and the men in my life, when the women we look to and love are striving with their own energy and commitment to their highest callings. I'm sorry if you do not agree, but this has been true in my life without fail for the more than fifty years I've been breathing my own oxygen.

It is also true that I do my very best to love folks with viewpoints different from my own, including those who have chosen homosexuality. I disagree with their lifestyle choice, to be sure, but I certainly don't hate them, and I don't chase after them with my beliefs. I love them enough to tell them the truth should they ask, but that's it. It might surprise some to learn that I have friends who practice homosexuality. Some years ago, at least once per week, I visited a man in a county home who had foolishly left his wife and daughter to pursue the "liberation" of homosexuality, liberation that took his life. Weekly I listened to his story and attempted to encourage his prodigal return before AIDS killed him. I watched him wane from a seemingly healthy man into a skeleton with breath in a matter of months. Disagree if you wish, but please abandon any claims of misogyny and homophobia. They have no basis here.

Disagreement need not equate to hate.

Back on point, these days there is little doubt that masculinity is under attack. Since at least the 1960s, our culture has been trying to dissolve men, to discredit the honorable men who formed this country, chastise the brave men who've protected it, and castrate the contemporary men who are striving to support, restore, and lead it. Certainly, there have been beacons of hope here and there, but far-left politicians, extreme feminists, and the gender confused arrive quickly on the scene in an attempt to extinguish the flickers before they cast light.

In her excellent opinion journal "Welcome Back, Duke," published in the *Wall Street Journal* in October 2001, Peggy Noonan spoke of strong men who protect, haul, lead, and rebuild, masculine men for whom there emerged a welcome admiration through the 9/11 haze: "We are experiencing a new respect for their old-fashioned masculinity, a new respect for physical courage, for strength and for the willingness to use both for the good of others." That was twenty years ago.

Just twelve years ago, in 2009, Dockers brand released an advertising campaign inviting men to rediscover masculinity. Their "Wear The Pants" campaign boldly put forth a truth-filled "Manifesto." It was rightly critical of our culture's attempt to cast aside traditional masculinity in favor of latte-sipping grown boys joyfully inclined toward androgyny. Dockers correctly acknowledged that "there are questions our genderless society has no answers for." Clearly recognizing that communities often implode, families break down, and children rage without a masculine hand to guide them, ad writers called men to step up to the plate and be strong, heroic men—to once again "wear the pants." That was twelve years ago.

Instances of support for traditional masculinity have been but flashes in the proverbial pan in this age. We seem to have forgotten the inconvenient truths from the aftermath of 9/11 now that the dust has settled, and construction crews, composed mostly of men, have cleared the rubble and constructed something of beauty in its place. We've once again tossed our crosses and cursed our flag as though ashamed to be Americans. We protest in our streets with hands outstretched, many of those sign-holding hands apparently unable to work. In less than twelve years, Dockers changed their tune 180° to abandon the rugged male. Now owned by Levi Strauss & Co., once an icon of rough-and-tumble America, Dockers now proudly partners with Stonewall Community Foundation to champion LGBTQ+ rights.

Manhood has been made the fool by womanizing "leaders" such as Bill Clinton, profane, buffoonish screen princes of "reality" TV, and mainstream media bent on portraying men either as proud, healthy, successful homosexuals or as ignorant, incompetent, cowering grown boys. In 2018, the insurance company Progressive showed character Jamie nearly wetting himself with astonishment when heroine Flo and a mysterious computer emerge from behind secret doors. To conclude the stomach-turning display, Jamie literally squeals with excitement at the surprise appearance of his mommy. Though I don't recommend it, feel free to watch it for yourself if you think I'm off base. Searching with something like "Progressive TV commercial real actors" will likely get you there. These examples and media portrayals are not what men and manhood are intended to be, and they don't represent what most men are. It's time to fight back.

> It's time to forsake your phone, abandon toxic social media, turn off the TV, drop the video games, get off the couch, work up some sweat and blood in the arena of your calling, and show our young men of today what being a faithful, strong, confident, godly man is all about.

I have never attended a funeral where a man's moral depravity, lack of faith, lack of virtue, physical weakness, or inclination toward cowardice were ever applauded. Deep down, we admire and celebrate the faith, masculinity, and strong character traits of our fathers, grandfathers, forefathers, and comic superheroes. We train our Special Forces for the worst and breathe sighs of relief and pride when their missions in defense of our peace and freedom are bravely and masterfully executed. Unfortunately, in many homes, schools, and communities today, folks are afraid or embarrassed to encourage the same spirit and strengths in their boys. Healthy competition is thwarted; everybody gets a ribbon, regardless of merit; and traditional, biblical perspectives are silenced for fear of exclusion or offense. This is cowardly, foolish, and dangerous. It is not the way the world works, and it will lead to our downfall. Let's put a stop to it. By doing our part to develop and support strong, faithful, courageous, capable young men of substance, we have the power to effect positive change.

It is admirable to be a man among men, eager to listen, calculated in speech, proudly developing broad shoulders, thick skin, a robust spine, and a love of God, country, and women as complementary equals. It's okay to be strong, courageous, faithful, chivalrous, and full of virility, and it's okay to develop one's position of leadership and authority. With all my vices, weaknesses, and shortcomings, this is who I strive to be. It's who we want our daughters to marry and our sons to become. Such is the man most capable of complementing his wife and encouraging her to become the woman she has every right to be. The man you are becoming need not cower at the altar of groupthink and popular decadence.

*The man or woman you become is a result of
your daily choices. Choose wisely.*

I applaud and thank the Kendrick brothers, Bryan Fischer, Abraham Hamilton III, Orrin C. Hudson, Dave Ramsey, Dr. David Jeremiah, and others with similar courage and purpose to swim against the popular and political current. These leaders accurately portray praiseworthy men and women on our screens, over our airways, and in our culture. With my words, I'm sure I have signed myself up to be simultaneously loved and hated. "It's okay; it's what we've got to do" rings in my ear. It is a price I am willing to pay, and it would be an honor to walk similar paths as those listed above. Many before us have paid a much greater price for the opportunities and freedoms we enjoy. In their honor and memory, I gladly lock arms with those of kindred spirit. You'll find us standing proudly before our flag and kneeling humbly before our Creator, never the other way around.

Regarding Point 3, I want to teach our sons and other young men as my father taught me. As you have read and surely come to understand, I am very fortunate to have Paul Geswein as my father. I try not to take that fact for granted. I work hard every day to be the best father I can be to each of our children just as he has been for me.

*A child needs a father, a mother, and a safe, united, loving
home. This is the best way. It is the way God intended.*

Sadly, many homes are missing one or more of these important elements. Too often, hardworking mothers are left to raise children alone for reasons too numerous to dive into here. In many cases, the dads are just deadbeats, nothing more than seed donors.

Boys need fathers in a special way just as girls need mothers in their own special way. Many things are more effectively caught than taught, and, with no father in the home, young boys are too often left with tragic experiential gaps in spite of a single mom's best efforts. I intend to do my part to help young boys who are not so fortunate to be growing up in a unified, loving home with an engaged father.

After some years of deliberation and planning, in the fall of 2018, I hosted my first-ever camp for young boys. We affectionately called our event *Man Camp* (not to be mistaken for the goofy comedy program of the same name that emerged in 2019). Our Man Camp is a skills and leadership camp for young boys between the ages of about eleven and fourteen. Man Camp is intended to teach and empower young boys to become the strong, skillful, godly young men our world needs.

We read Scripture. We talk about challenges in our culture and what part each of us can play in addressing these challenges. We open doors for ladies, start huge brush fires without matches, and navigate the night woods without lights and without fear. We cook our own meals and clean up after ourselves. We say, "Please," and, "Thank you." We work hard and serve others. We operate equipment and chainsaws. We change oil, rotate tires, mow grass, and chop wood. We attend church, sleep well, and make no excuses for being genuine males. Two more camps were held in 2019 and one in 2020 in spite of COVID-19. Lord willing, many more will happen in the coming years. We will not reach everyone, but we will reach someone.

"It's better to build boys than mend men."
—S. Truett Cathy, former CEO of Chick-fil-A

PRIMITIVE RAFT CONSTRUCTION, MAN CAMP 2020

Equipment maintenance, Man Camp 2020

Service work, Man Camp 2020

INTERRUPTING OUR BICYCLE TREK FOR A PHOTO IN
FRONT OF A FITTING MESSAGE, MAN CAMP 2020

To move forward with camps and this mission to train young men, I need help. I need partnership, guidance, financial and legal support, and the experience of others. In the coming months, I will be holding more camps, developing strategies, and seeking sponsors, partners, and kindred spirits to help advance this cause.

If you are encouraged, excited, and stirred to action by this concept and would like to be involved in some way, I would love to hear from you.

Back now to you. If you haven't made your list yet, please do so right now. A quick and dirty version of your list can be knocked out in ten minutes if you really focus. Remember, it need not be perfect; it just needs to *be*. It needs to exist.

Please take action and follow through. Even without
knowing you, I know you have much to offer.

From Dr. David Jeremiah, I have heard it said, "A man of God in the will of God is immortal until His work is done." I find that statement both true and comforting. It also goes without saying that such a statement applies equally to women.

We all have divine assignments to complete, and we are not going anywhere until we've completed His work. I know God's work for me is not yet done, and I have zero fear of death. If you are reading these words, His work for you isn't done, either. Please join me in appreciating and thanking those folks who have helped us along our way and please join your hand with mine in striving to leave this world better than we found it.

> "Be such a man, and live such a life, that if every man were such as you, and every life a life like yours, this earth would be God's paradise." —Phillips Brooks

In closing, I encourage you to watch the movie *Secondhand Lions*, often. You'll see why it fits so properly into this collection, and you'll recall and appreciate Hub McCann's words from one of the movie's greatest scenes. In this scene, Hub is giving his young nephew Walter a portion of his "what every boy needs to know about being a man" speech:

> Sometimes the things that may or may not be true are the things that a man needs to believe in the most: that people are basically good; that honor, courage, and virtue mean everything; that power and money, money and power, mean nothing; that good always triumphs over evil. And, I want you to remember this, that love, true love, never dies. You remember that, boy. You remember that. Doesn't matter if they're true or not, you see. A man should believe in those things because those are the things worth believing in. Yeah. Got that?

Thanks, Hub!

Mom, I look forward to sharing this book with you someday, perhaps others, as well. Thank you for being a great mom, for planting and nurturing, for everything.

Professor Carvill, would you have ever guessed? Thank you for forcing me to read the first of now so many books, starting in your class,

Twentieth-Century American Novels. I hope you appreciate this one and relish perhaps some sliver of credit for its existence. I have no idea if you agree or disagree with the lessons I've highlighted or the positions I've taken. I suppose it doesn't really matter. Agree or disagree, I learned more from you and your class at Rose than you might have suspected. I really appreciate your contribution. Thank you.

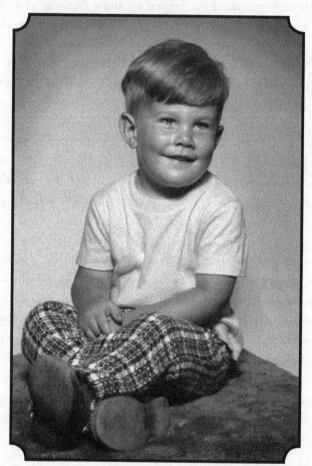

ONE OF DAD'S FAVORITE PHOTOS OF ME, CIRCA 1972

"Son, if it is worth doing, it is worth doing right. Do your best." I did my best, Dad. Thanks for being a great dad.

Love and prayers,
Son number two

POSTSCRIPT

Your Reflections, Your Contributions

I HOPE THIS BOOK OF REFLECTIONS AND LESSONS HAS BEEN HELPFUL OR inspiring to you in some way. I hope that the actions you have taken after reading this book have made your life and the lives of those around you better.

I would like to hear from you. Perhaps another book, or a series of follow-up books, should emerge from the feedback and personal testimony you share with me. It would be a great honor for me to collect, package, and share your reflections and testimony to inspire others and help to rebuild a broken world.

Perhaps additional stories from female readers and reflections from lives of inspirational women will be shared along with those I fully expect from men. There are so many paths the next leg of this adventure could follow. I am excited about the journey. I thank you once again for having read this book. I look forward to hearing your feedback. Together, we can contribute, improve, inspire, and leave legacies of eternal value.

Please use the pages that follow to commit your reflections, your resolutions, your actions, and your testimonies to paper. I look forward to hearing from you.

NOTES

Chapter 2

1   Dr. Emerson Eggerichs, *Love & Respect: The Love She Most Desires, The Respect He Desperately Needs* (Nashville, TN: W Publishing Group, 2004), 194–196.

Chapter 7

1   Admiral William H. McRaven, *Make Your Bed: Little Things that Can Change Your Life...and Maybe the World* (New York: Grand Central Publishing, 2017), 38.

Chapter 16

1   Booker T. Washingon, *Up from Slavery* (CreateSpace Independent Publishing Platform, 2015), 91.
2   Peggy Noonan, "Welcome Back, Duke," Opinion Journal, *Wall Street Journal*, October 12, 2001.
3   Kelly Crawford, "The Call for Men to Wear the Pants: Dockers' Manifesto," *GenerationCedar.com*, December 10, 2009.